SOFIA SOULI

D0478239

GREEK
MYTHOLOGY

EDITIONS
TOUBI'S ®
ΕΚΔΟΣΕΙΣ

Textes: SOFIA SOULI
Translation: PHILIP RAMP
Artistic supervision: NORA DRAMITINOU - ANASTASOGLOU

Typesetting, colour separations, editing, publising: M. TOUBIS GRAPHIC ART S.A.

Copyright © 1995 EDITIONS MICHALIS TOUBIS S.A.
519 Vouliagmenis Av., Ilioupoli 163 41, Tel. (01) 9923876, Fax: (01) 9923867 - Athens

1
CREATION OF THE GODS

The birth of the gods - The first gods - The Titans -
The battle of the Titans - The battle of the Giants - The human race
8 - 19

2
THE GODS

The twelve Gods of Olympus - The lesser gods -
Other inferior gods - The oracles
20 - 61

3
THE HEROES

Heracles - Theseus - The voyage of the Argonauts - Perseus -
Bellerophon - Daedalus and Icarus - Orpheus - Phaethon
62 - 123

4
THE TROJAN WAR

Its causes
The Achaean Campaign Against Troy - The Trojan Horse
124 - 149

5
THE ODYSSEY

The wanderings of Odysseus -
The return to Ithaca
150 - 167

Complete index of names   pag. 171

MYTHOLOGY

A GREEK WORD

ntellect is the gift of the human race, the greatest and most enduring of all time. This is the means by which it perceives, exists, creates and evolves. No matter how extensive knowledge is, it has its limits. Intellect thirsts for fulfillment, to ceaselessly push these limits outward. Thus, people in that far-off period wanted to learn for they felt powerless and vulnerable in a world without bounds. They were deeply concerned with the beginning and the end and all the supernatural forces that could not be mastered. Through intellect, humanity came to fashion its view of the world. Utilizing the raw information from its immediate surroundings, it cultivated knowledge and experience, while imagination filled in the rest. Mankind had need of "myth" because that was his own personal truth. His faith in this increased his certitude about the world he had created around himself. This is how we have come to accept the myth in its conventional sense, that is, a narration that informs us about an older order of the world and explains it.

The content of Greek mythology is not a simple matter. There is a practically endless series of accounts from various periods, and derivations on which enormous classificatory endeavor has been expended and that is only the beginning. Even more research was required to cross-reference and parallel mythical and/or historical events and narrations in order to validate them. This may seem strange, but Greek myth is not entirely a "fairy tale". It is a representation of certain far-off periods and helps fill in the gaps in history, but above all else it indicates the level that a culture had achieved.

Manners and customs, religion and the superstitions of a people that had a historical presence for thousands of years before, is not a "myth" in any sense. Because, though the gods and the incredible encounters

of the heroes with supernatural beings may have been the creations of fantasy, they arose from a fundamental truth that told one then, and tells one now, that a certain number of people in this corner of the world, many centuries before the advent of Christ, were building cities, subduing natural forces and foreign nations, setting off to unknown parts, founding colonies, leading art to great heights and cultivating the body and the spirit. All this was being done by the Greeks alone!

When one speaks of the Cyclopian walls of the Mycenaean period, one immediately understands that the myth came to exist because the work was such a superhuman achievement for the period, it seemed these walls could have only been created by giants such as the Cyclopses.

The stirring narrations of Homer are not merely the product of a cultural heritage and the imagination of people who lived three thousand years before. Let us never forget how the world was left speechless when the excavations at Troy and Mycenae brought to light proof of his account of their cultural magnificence, the wars they fought and the heroes who fought them, all before 1200 B.C.! The Troy of Priam emerged with its walls and its sanctuaries, while the "rich in gold Mycenaeans" as Homer refers to them, and the tombs of Atreaus and Agamemnon, also laden with gold, came to light.

The word mythology is Greek and has been adopted by other languages, sharing the universal values of this wealth that has survived right down to the present.

This golden heritage of Homer, Hesiod, the great tragic and lyric writers of antiquity, as well as so many others from that period, is the pride of the Greek people. Because without this, European education as we know it would not exist; without this worldwide literature would today be a much poorer thing.

1

CREATION OF THE GODS

BIRTH OF THE GODS - FIRST GODS - THE TITANS - BATTLE OF THE TITANS - BATTLE OF THE GIANTS - HUMAN RACE

The ancient Greeks with their brilliant and imaginative spirit created a complete order of things that functioned harmoniously in the infinite world that contained them. The beginning and the genesis of this world occupied them in the same way it did the early people of every civilization. Thus, they interpreted natural forces and unexplained phenomena in what they considered a reasonable way, true to a system of laws which arose from a respect for the superior beings who defined and ruled the universe. The stimuli from the environment and the incredible vastness they saw around them made these early people, in what is now called Greece, deify abstract concepts, elements of nature and all the other amazing things they believed regulated their fortunes and their survival.

But the divinity that was worshipped above all others during prehistoric times (and not only in Greece but among nearly all peoples) was Mother Earth. Those far-off people trod the surface of the earth and were nourished by its fruits. For Mediterranean people,

Clay figurine of the divine mother.

Mother Earth was frequently identified with the goddess of fertility; the first idols from that period, also found in Greece, depict this female figure with naked, full breasts and a disproprotionately large pelvis, a typical sign of fertility. The cultivation of the earth was clearly connected to religious practices.

A knowledge of these early gods will reveal that they evolved along with Greek thought. The sceptre of the lords of the world changed hands until the most powerful came to dominate. The battles of the Titans and the Giants gave rise to a new generation of gods who then gained control. Together with these gods, the human race took its first halting steps and right from the very start paid the price for its weakness, even though its fate had already been determined by these very gods.

Starting with the first gods and goddesses, one arrives at those that prevailed and that are better known. The names of some of them will be mentioned only because the great protagonists of the following chapters came from them: the Greek gods and heroes.

THE FIRST GODS

very tale and every truth involved with the creation of the universe has always begun with Chaos. Therefore, Chaos was also deified in the birth of the ancient Greek world. Erebus and Night were originally born of Chaos and their children were Air and Day. Dark Night also gave birth to Death, Sleep, Dreams and the Fates and even the Hesperides and Eris. Then Mother Earth became the wide and stable base from which all life sprang. The Sky, which enveloped it with its immensity, was the greatest god at the beginning of the world.

THE TITANS

other Earth was the leading protagonist in cosmogony. It formed a union with Sky to make the first divine couple. From this union the Titans were born:

The first born **Oceanus** fathered with **Tethys** the Rivers and the Oceanids.

Hyperion and **Theia** sired Helios (The Sun), Selene (The Moon) and Eos (Dawn). **Coeus** and **Phoebe** gave birth to Leto and Asteria.

Creius married **Eurybia** (the daughter of Mother Earth and Pondus) and produced Astraeus, Pallas and Perses.

Iapetus, who coupled with the Oceanid **Clymene** (daughter of Oceanus and Tethys) sired Atlas, Menoetius, Prometheus and Epimetheus.

Finally, **Cronus** and **Rhea,** the Titan and the Titaness, brought into the world those destined to be its future rulers. This couple gave birth to Demeter, Hestia, Hera, Hades, Poseidon and Zeus who later shared their power and ruled the world.

Zeus ruled the sky, Poseidon the sea and Hades (Pluto) the underworld.

Aitheras ("Air") the son of Night and Erebus was the personification of delicate and brilliant, ethereal matter, living and divine. The ancients believed it hung suspended above the air that enveloped Mother Earth.

Asia,
the daughter of Oceanus and Tethys, gave her name to the well-known continent. Asia is identified with, or confused with, Clymene. From her marriage to the Titan Iapetus were born Atlas, Prometheus, Epimetheus and Menoetius.

Other Children of the Earth
Besides the Titans, which we have already referred to among the divine couples, Mother Earth also gave birth to Thetis and Mnemosyne. The Cyclopses and the Hundred-handed ones were monstrous children who were born much later while the hugely powerful Antaeus is mentioned as her son by Poseidon.

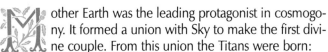

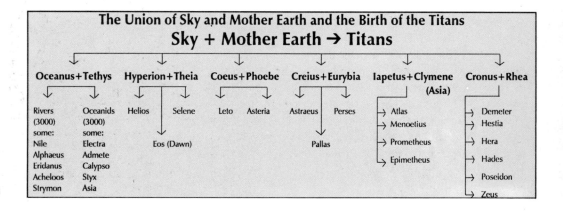

The Union of Sky and Mother Earth and the Birth of the Titans

Sky + Mother Earth → Titans

Oceanus+Tethys		Hyperion+Theia		Coeus+Phoebe		Creius+Eurybia		Iapetus+Clymene (Asia)	Cronus+Rhea
Rivers (3000) some: Nile Alphaeus Eridanus Acheloos Strymon	Oceanids (3000) some: Electra Admete Calypso Styx Asia	Helios	Selene → Eos (Dawn)	Leto	Asteria	Astraeus → Pallas	Perses	→ Atlas → Menoetius → Prometheus → Epimetheus	→ Demeter → Hestia → Hera → Hades → Poseidon → Zeus

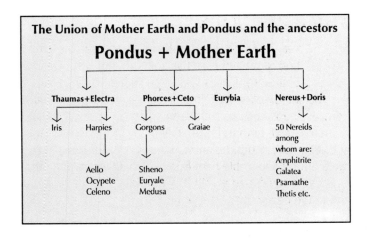

The Union of Mother Earth and Pondus and the ancestors

Pondus + Mother Earth

Thaumas+Electra		Phorces+Ceto		Eurybia	Nereus+Doris
Iris	Harpies	Gorgons	Graiae		50 Nereids among whom are: Amphitrite
	Aello Ocypete Celeno	Stheno Euryale Medusa			Calatea Psamathe Thetis etc.

The Nereids

Oceanus had fifty grandchildren (and maybe even one hundred, according to another view), daughters of Nereus and Doris who personified the waves of the sea. These Nereids lived at the bottom of the sea in the palace of their father and spent their day swimming and playing with the dolphins, or sitting on golden thrones singing and weaving. The most well known of them were Amphitrite, Thetis (the future mother of the hero Achilles) Psamathe (mother of Aeacus) and Galatea.

In the beginning Sky and Mother Earth were united but they later separated. After the Sky (Uranus) was mutilated by its terrible child Cronus, Mother Earth formed a union with **Pondus** and their union brought into the world **Thaumas, Phorces, Ceto, Eurybia** and **Nereus.** The union between Thaumas and the Oceanid **Electra** gave birth to Iris and the fearful Harpies (Aello, Thyella, Ocypete) whom we shall encounter below. Phorces and Ceto gave birth to the two Graiae (who were old women from birth) and the fearsome Gorgons: Stheno, Euryale and Medusa. Nereus and the Oceanid **Doris,** had fifty daughters, the Nereids.

Cronus and Rhea

Cronus, a member of the first generation of gods, was the only son of Mother Earth to help her in taking revenge on his father Uranus (Sky). After castrating Uranus, Cronus took his place and cast his brothers, the **Hundred-handed** Ones and the **Cyclopes,** into Tartarus - where their father had already imprisoned them. Then Cronus married his sister Rhea, but tried to ensure that none of their children would live, as his parents had told him that he would lose power to one of his own offspring. As soon as the children were born, Cronus devoured them: Hestia, Demeter, Hera, Pluto (Hades) and Poseidon, one after the other. As soon as Rhea realised she was pregnant again (with Zeus), she fled to Crete and bore the baby secretly. She left the baby to be brought up by the Oceanid Metis, giving Cronus a stone wrapped in swaddling-clothes which he took to be the newborn child and ate. So it happened that Zeus was saved.

Rhea delivering the swaddled stone in the place of Zeus to her husband and brother. (160 A.D., Rome, Museo Capitolino).

11

THE BATTLE OF THE TITANS

The Titanesses Theia, Rhea, Themis, Mnemosyne, Phoebe and Tethys, even though they coupled with their brother Titans to give birth to various classes of divnities, did not take the side of these brothers in the Battle of the Titans.

As soon as Zeus grew up, he forced Cronus to swallow a potion which made him vomit up all the children he had swallowed. All the brothers and sisters then joined forces to liberate the Hundred-handed Ones and the Cyclopses, and they declared war on Cronus, whose allies were his brothers the Titans. All the gods, young and old, took part in this war, the awe-inspiring Battle of the Titans. During the fighting, the Titans had their camp on Mt. Othrys, while Zeus and his allies occupied neighbouring Mt. Olympus.

The Cyclopses gave Zeus thunder, lightning and the thunderbolt; to Poseidon they gave a trident, and to Hades they gave a helmet of darkness. The three Hundred-handed ones, with their three hundred hands, hurled huge rocks at the Titans. Victory for the gods of Olympus was swift, and so Zeus, a younger deity, came to succeed an earlier and more primitive generation of gods. He was wiser, with superior values, and he represented the forces of nature.

Not all the members of the generation of the Titans, however, had been on the side of Cronus. Oceanus, for example, did not support him, while some sources say that Prometheus, son of Iapetus, did much to help Zeus. After the conclusion of the Battle of the Titans, Cronus and his brothers were bound in chains and flung into Tartarus, where the Hundred-handed ones stayed to stand guard over them.

Atlas

For some mythical figures the new order of things which now prevailed had painful consequences. Atlas, for example, one of the sons of the Titan Iapetus, was severely punished for his part in the war against Zeus. He was sent west to the ends of the earth, where lie the borders of Night, the the child Chaos, and where the Hesperides guard their golden apples, as we shall see shortly. There he was doomed to stay, forever holding up the sky over the earth, or the earth and sky together, or the axis of the earth. According to another myth, Atlas has formerly been the king of a fairy tale realm beyond the Ocean - a land called Atlantis.

Atlas had seven daughters by Pleione, the Pleiades: Taygete, Electra, Alcyone, Asterope, Celaeno, Maia and Merope. After their death the Pleiades formed a constellation in the sky.

Atlas condemned to bear the Earth on his shoulders. (Later Roman period, National Museum of Naples, Italy).

THE BATTLE OF THE GIANTS

hen Zeus punished the Titans, Mother Earth was angry that some of her children had been punished in this way (or, according to another version, because she did not think the gods were doing her enough honour). To take her revenge, she gave birth to the Giants.

Design for the north frieze of the altar of Zeus at Pergamon, depicting Fate, the ally of Zeus, struggling with a hideous Giant

The Giants were not immortal despite their divine origins. But to be killed they had to be simultaneously attacked by a god and a mortal. That is why Heracles took part in the Battle of the Giants. In order to save her children, Mother Earth grew an herb that protected them. But before the Giants had a chance to make use of it, Zeus cut it off and took it away.

On the opposite page: A Giant, naked with a helmet, fighting with a lion. (From the north frieze at the Treasury of the Siphnians at Delphi, 525 B.C., Delphi, Archaeological Museum).

The Giants were huge creatures with the hair of snakes and bodies whose lowrer parts were those of dragons. Their appearance inspired terror, and they were almost invincible. As soon as they were born they launched their attack on the gods of Olympus, hurling lighted torches, a rain of boulders and entire flaming trees. The mountains shook, and the air and sea were a hell of fire. The Olympian gods were thus forced to go to war once more, with Zeus and his thunderbolts in command, flanked by comrades capable of standing any test: Poseidon, Apollo, Hephaestus, the Fates, Dionysus and his retinue, and all the others. But the leading role in this battle was played by Athena, who was born during the course of the war, springing fully-armed from the head of Zeus. She immediately killed the Giant Pallas and took up her position by her father's side. The Battle of the Giants was prolonged, and would never have ended if Fate had not fulfilled itself as a mortal and fought side by side with the gods to bring them victory. This was Heracles, with whose help the Giants were killed off one by one.

Zeus duelling with the terrible demon Typhon who had been sent by Mother Earth to avenge the death of her children, the Titans. (Chalcidice hydria, 540-530 B.C., Munich).

THE HUMAN RACE

Once, in very early times when there were only immortal gods and no mortal beings in the world, it occurred to the immortals that they might create such beings to inhabit the earth. When this was done, Zeus ordered Prometheus and Epimetheus, sons of the Titan Iapetus, to endow the creatures of the earth with gifts and powers.

Epimetheus asked of his brother that he should be allowed to share out the gifts of the gods. He bestowed beauty on one animal, strength on another, agility to counterbalance another's smallness of size, intelligence to offset yet another's bulk. And so Epimetheus went on giving out, decorating and sharing - yet he lacked the wisdom of his brother, for he gave all his gifts and weapons to the members of the animal kingdom and left man last, bare and defenceless, with no natural weapons.

Prometheus

Prometheus, the friend of man, stole wisdom from Athena and gave man reason, to square the balance. Then he stole fire from the forge of Hephaestus and gave it to man as a gift. Since that time, man has had fire to keep himself warm and alive, and to help him create. Prometheus became the protector of the human race, and taught it all he knew. But this angered Zeus, who did not want mankind to be helped to resemble the gods. And when he discovered that Prometheus had given man fire, he unleashed his thunder and lightning: until that time, fire had been reserved for the gods. Prometheus' punishment was a harsh one. Zeus chained him to a peak in the Caucasus, at the end of the world, where an eagle swooped down on him every day and pecked out his liver. But during the night Prometheus' liver grew back again, and so the next day he would undergo his torment once more. Thirty years were to pass before Heracles released Prometheus from his terrible ordeal.

A variation of this myth gives another explanation for Zeus' anger with Prometheus. Once during a formal sacrifice Prometheus divided up the ox, which was to be sacrificed, in a very deceptive way: on the one side he put all the lean meat and the entrails hidden under the hide of the animal and on the other all the bones covered in fat. When it was offered to Zeus he chose the portion with the fat. But when he learned that his portion was nothing but bones while humans got all the meat he fell into a rage and took fire away from them, which Prometheus later stole back.

The first human races
During the reign of Cronus, Hesiod mentions there was a Gold Race of human beings. Life then was pure pleasure because people lived without problems, happy as gods. They had no cares and there was no old age. They were always young, amused themselves constantly and ate only the fruits of the Earth because they had nothing to hide nor did anyone steal. When people were tired of living they lay down and slept sweetly. Then their bodies became transparent and light and a simple breeze would carry them off to a land of peace and magic. After the Gold Race came the Silver Race which was not as happy as the previous one and people began to break the law. The kingdom of the gods also changed hands then. Things became even worse with the Bronze Race when disasters, illnesses, violence and wars began. The heroes then made their appearance for they were necessary. With the Iron Race, people came to live a nearly unbearable life, struggling day in and day out to survive with hope the only thing to hold on to.

On the opposite page, above: Heracles arriving unexpectedly to liberate Pometheus. (Early Attican kratar. Design circa 610 B.C., Athens, Archaeological Museum).

(Laconian cylix, 550 B.C., Rome, Vatican Museum).

The torture of two Titans. Atlas lifting the sky with great effort and Prometheus tormented by an eagle which is tearing at his chest.

17

Pandora

The destiny of Pandora

The radiantly beautiful Pandora, a divine gift from Zeus to Epimetheus had as her destiny the punishment of the human race for the initiative Prometheus took in giving it fire: the properties of fire are of a divine force and people had to pay dearly for their acquisition.

ephaestus the smith, the god of fire, made the first woman in his forge. To begin with, she was a metal statue, but she was so beautiful that Zeus decided to give her life. All the other gods bestowed gifts upon her: beauty, grace, intelligence, skill and persuasiveness. But Hermes also gave her cunning and falsehood and Hera gave her the curiosity which would never let her rest.

Zeus sent Pandora to Epimetheus as a gift. He was so delighted by her beauty that he took her as his wife. As a wedding present, they were given a handsome box decorated with precious stones and gold. The box was locked, but Zeus gave the couple the key - saying to Pandora that if she wished to live happily with her husband, she should never open the box.

For a while, Epimetheus and Pandora lived quietly and happily together. But the curiosity which Hera had made part of Pandora's character proved to be more powerful in the end, and one day she opened the box. Out flew all the miseries and misfortunes which have afflicted man since: disease, despair, pain and all the other evils. But last of all came hope, like a little bird bearing a message of consolation for mankind.

Design depicting Pandora caught between the mallets of the Seleni.

Hephaestus made Pandora of earth and water, beautiful as a goddess, and Athena dressed and ornamented her. In this depiction Pandora is called Anesidora and both of them are old names for the Earth with its bountiful gifts. (Interior of cylix, 470-460 B.C., London, British Museum).

Deucalion and Pyrrha

The time came when man turned evil, and there was nothing right or beautiful in what he did. Zeus decided to punish the human race by drowning it in a flood. But in order to ensure it would survive, he chose Deucalion and Pyrrha who were the only good people. Pyrrha was the daughter of Epimetheus and Pandora. Zeus sent rain which fell for nine days and nights, swamping all the towns and cities. When it was over, Deucalion and Pyrrha, who had saved themselves in an ark, sacrificed to the gods to thank them. Then they followed Zeus' instructions in order to create a new human race.

After covering their faces, they began to walk forward, dropping stones behind them but not looking round. Men sprang up from the stones which Deucalion dropped, and women from those left by Pyrrha. The couple also had children of their own, who were regarded as the offspring of Zeus: Hellen, Amphictyon, Protogenia, Melanthia, Thyea and Pandora.

Hellen, their first-born, was regarded as the forefather of the Hellenes (Greeks).

2
THE GODS

TWELVE GODS OF OLYMPUS -
LESSER GODS - OTHER INFERIOR GODS - ORACLES

The ancient divinities we have referred to, at a certain point no longer satisfied the imagination or the yearnings of religion. People then wanted more actively involved gods to keep them company in their daily lives and to take a position in regard to their problems. Thus, the victors of Olympus grew large in their imagination and came to rule over religious worship. So powerful and the same time so vulnerable to human weaknesses, they regulated the fortunes and the lives of those they both loved and

Repoduction of the gold and ivory statue of Zeus, one of the seven wonders of the ancient world.

hated. Splendid, magnificent, each one with his own character, they became objects of worship for many centuries.

These gods shared all of mankind's virtues and faults. They were severe, punishing every unjust act, while protecting and assisting the just and the pious. They even had their own likes and dislikes which governed their behaviour toward mortals. This was made very clear during the Trojan War when the Olympian gods got involved and assisted either Achaeans or Trojans, depending on whom each of them favoured. They were vengeful but also excessively generous, while at the same time being propitiated by the material

sacrifices they were offered by the faithful. Animals were slaughtered and burnt on the altars and the fruits of the earth offered. There was even human sacrifice though this was usually in vain because it put a great strain on human faith.

There was no job or social need that was not connected to the worship of some god: from farming to education, from the fine arts to hunting, from military valour to love. Here one finds certain gods more carefree and fun-loving, who gave life its necessary zest with their high spirits and merriment; this facet is to be found in the religious worship of Dionysus, Pan and Aphrodite.

An endeavor will be made to present the gods that made up the Pantheon of Olympus and then to mention the lesser gods who are also of great interest.

Even more minor deities will be mentioned as Greek mythology personified all human concepts and emotions.

Thus, having become acquainted with the distinctive characteristics of each god, we will be better able to understand their presence and participation in the adventures of the heroes we will encounter below.

The gods were worshipped with ceremonies and the dedication of objects. The faithful sought the favour of a god by means of a ceremony conducted by priests and priestesses. These figures have dedicated their life to worshipping. The god of the temple to which they belonged. A priest and priestess are standing in an attitude of prayer befor the inscribed column in the illustration.

THE TWELVE GODS OF OLYMPUS

Olympus, the highest Greek mountain and lying in Macedonia, was the residence of the Olympian gods and above all else the throne of Zeus. In his epics Homer mentions the heavenly dwelling of the gods and dramatizes a variety of scenes in the apartments of each one of them. It was a great honour, even for the gods, to be found deserving of being received on Olympus and even more of one to actually be invited to reside there. The demi-god Heracles was so accepted, a sign of the very great respect all the gods had for him.

After gaining power over earth and heaven, the twelve gods of Olympus shared out responsibilities and posts amongst themselves in accordance with the wishes of Zeus. They lived on Mt. Olympus, the highest mountain in Greece, but they often came down and mingled with human beings, to help them, to punish them, to regulate their fortunes and even to unite with them and give birth to children. The children born of gods and mortals were called demi-gods, and they possessed rare skills. They performed a whole host of heroic feats and were admired by all.

The food of the gods was called ambrosia and their drink nectar - a drink reserved for them alone. But they willingly accepted the sacrifices and offerings of men, with animals slaughtered or burned to honour them or in the shape of the other fruits of the earth. The gods kept their promises, especially when made under oath. Their most fearful oath was that sworn "by the waters of the Styx". When a god swore on the waters of the Styx, the holy river, then it was sure he would never break his oath.

Depiction of a gathering of the Olympian gods.

Poseidon, Apollo and Artemis in the assembly of the gods from the east frieze of the Parthenon. (440 B.C., Athens, Parthenon Museum).

The gods of Olympus were almost omnipotent, in the sense that the power of each stopped where the jurisdiction of another began, since each had his or her own realm of power. Only Zeus was truly omnipotent. The gods resembled men in many ways. They had the same weaknesses, the same passions and the same emotions. They could become angry, jealous or envious, and they could love or fall in love just like men. But above all they demanded respect and honour from men.

The twelve gods occupied a special position in the religious consciousness of the ancient Greek world: "by the twelve gods of Olympus" was a sacred oath which demonstrated the respect the Greeks felt for these figures who determined the fate of the world and all those in it. Let us now get to know them a little better. The names of the twelve gods of Olympus were: Zeus, Hera, Athena, Poseidon, Demeter, Apollo, Artemis, Hermes, Ares, Aphrodite, Hephaestus and Hestia.

The Styx was a river in the underworld which, according to Hesiod, was a child of Oceanus and Tethys. During the Battle of the Giants, Styx with her children Zelus ("zeal"), Nike ("victory"), Cratos ("power") and Bia ("strength") helped the Olympian gods and Zeus to their triumphant outcome. For this service Zeus granted her the privilege of having the gods take oaths with her waters. Indeed, when it was necessary to commit some god to this heavy oath, Zeus sent Iris to the Styx to bring back a jug of water to Olympus. Styx was also the name of a spring in Arcadia which had awesome properties.

23

Gold stater with a representation of the head of Dodonian Zeus (334-331 B.C.).

ZEUS, the lord of of heaven and earth, the father of gods and humans

Zeus, the most powerful of the immortal Olympian gods, was born in the Diktaean cave and hidden by his mother Rhea in the Idaean cave on Crete, where he grew up on the milk provided by the goat Amaltheia and in the care of the Nymphs.

When he emerged triumphant among his brothers and the other gods, he acquired the respect and admiration of all. And when he won the wars of the Titans and Giants, he was justly accepted as the lord and father of all gods and men. His weapon was the thunderbolt, and his domain included both the earth and the sky. The lawful and perpetual wife of Zeus was Hera, who was always his steady, faithful companion in life and his works. The children of Zeus had countless love affairs with other goddesses and

The goat Amalthea

who nursed Zeus in the Idaean Cave was to many a Nymph. Out of gratitude the god endowed her horn with the ability to give its possessor all the good things he desired. The horn of Amalthea is synonymous with plenty.

The **Curetes** were demonic beings who were worshipped with orgiastic ceremonies and are identified with the Cabiri or the Corybantes. They were principally worshipped on Crete. Rhea assigned the guarding of the infant Zeus to them. So the cries of the baby would not reach the ears of Cronus, the Curetes danced around him and beat their spears on their shields thus covering up Zeus' cries.

Zeus with divine majesty, raises his terrible weapon, the thunderbolt. (Bronze statuette from Dodoni, 470 B.C., Athens, Archaeological Museum).

Drawing depicting Zeus on his chariot.

Zeus leads Ganymede to Olympus. Clay group. (480 B.C., Olympia, Archaeological Museum).

mortal women, often arousing the jealousy of Hera. In those relationships Zeus sired many other children, some of whom were gods, and others demi-gods and heroes. To mention just a few: the fruits of Zeus' relationship with Maia were Hermes, Semele and Dionysus; his offspring with Leto were Apollo and Artemis; he sired the Fates and the Hours on Themis, and he and Mnemosyne were the parents of the Nine Muses. The many love affairs which Zeus had with mortal women produced the demi-gods and heroes of which we shall have much to say later on.

Zeus loved and protected all his children, who often attracted the rage of Hera. Apart from the hundreds of women with whom, we are told, the father of gods and men enjoyed covert love relationships, we also know that Zeus was moved by the dynamic beauty of the young Ganymede, a member of the royal family of Troy. The boy was so handsome that he awoke the erotic interest of Zeus, who abducted him to Olympus to serve as his cup-bearer - that is, Ganymede's task was to make sure that Zeus' cup was always full of nectar.

Apart from his passions, in which respect, as we have seen, the gods resembled men, Zeus was the god who maintained the balance of justice. His role was not only to punish and avenge, but also to share in the pain of the unfortunate and help to relieve their sufferings by dispensing justice. The charismatic leaders of antiquity were described as "born of Zeus" or "nurtured by Zeus" when the speaker wished to praise the prudence of their government or their sense of justice.

Zeus and Europa

The beautiful Europa, the daughter of Agenora and Telephassa, was among the young women Zeus fell in love with. The maiden was playing with her girl friends on the shore at Sidon and her charms made the father of gods and men fall in love with her. In order to get near her he transformed himself into a pure white bull and went and lay at her feet.

As Europa took courage, she began to sport with the bull. But as soon as she sat on his back he leapt up and plunged into the sea. She cried for help in vain. The bull swam further and further from the shore.

Europa took firm hold of his horns to keep from falling off and in that way they reached Crete. At the spring of Gortys the couple made love under the shadow of the plane trees. Since that time the trees have never shed their leaves because they covered the love of a god. Zeus and Europa had three sons: the legendary Minos, the brave Sarpedon and the just Radamanthys. It is said that the bronze giant Talus, who guarded Crete and whom we shall meet later in the section on the Argonaut campaign, was a gift of Zeus to Europa.

Europa, who loved Zeus, gave her name to an entire continent. The world of the intellect and art has responded to the stimuli of this myth with true masterpieces. The "Abduction of Europa" was painted by Titian and Rembrandt and became a marvelous depiction by P. Veronese to ornament the palace of the Doges in Venice. Cellini was also inspired by the same subject and made a bronze group which is now in Rome.

Zeus transformed into a bull with Europa. (Krater, 450 B.C.).

Europa stayed on Crete, married its king Asterionas, who adopted her children and gave her name to a continent.

The bull whose shape Zeus assumed rose to heaven and became the well-known constellation of Taurus in the Zodiac cycle.

Cadmus, the founder of Thebes and the brother of Europa, came to Greece in quest of her.

Besides the Europa whom Zeus loved, there was the Oceanid Europa, the daughter of Oceanus and Tethys.

The abduction of Europa, a colour wood carving by the Greek engraver, K. Grammatopoulos (National Gallery).   27

Head of Hera (Circa 420 B.C., Athens, Archaeological Museum).

HERA, the patron goddess of the family and married women

Hera, the worthy spouse of Zeus, was the patron of marriage and married women. Her own relationship with Zeus long predated their marriage, and they used to meet in secret from their parents. But after the twelve gods took power and Zeus began to reign on Olympus, they were able to get married. Hera intervenes in many of the myths, and brought up numerous children apart from her own. She punished infidelity and took fierce revenge on her husband's paramours. When Leto became pregnant with Apollo and Artemis, Hera pursued her to Delos, then a floating island. She caused Io, whom Zeus loved deeply, to be transformed into a cow. The cult of Hera was especially strong at Argos, where she was, the patron goddess of the city. In the Trojan War, Hera took the Greek side and intervened actively in many ways, affecting the outcome of that war.

Hera in a lavish costume, regal crown and sceptre. (Interior of cylix, 470-460 B.C., Munich, Staatliche Antikensammlungen).

In the Battle of the Giants, Hera a attacking a giand (circa 525 B.C., Delphi, Archaeological Museum).

The birth of Athena from the head of Zeus.

The renowned "Athena the Beautiful", a Roman copy of the chryselephantine statue of the goddess, a work of the great sculptor Pheidias, found in the Parthenon.

ATHENA, the goddess of wisdom

After the victory of the Olympian gods in the Battle of the Titans, Zeus formed a union with Metis, daughter of Oceanus and Tithys. Her parents told Zeus that the fruit of the union would first be Athena, whose bravery and wisdom would rival those of her father, and later a son, who would be more clever than Zeus and might, one day, be a menace to his throne. Zeus responded by swallowing Metis. But the time for Athena to be born was drawing near, and so Zeus ordered Prometheus (or Hephaestus in some versions) to lay open his head with an axe. All were amazed to see Athena spring fully-armed from Zeus' head, brandishing her spear. The young goddess stood side by side with her father during the Battle of the Giants, where she managed to overcome Enceladus, casting him down and throwing the whole of Sicily on top of him to immobilise him. Although she was the goddess of war, she was not warlike. Clever and wise, she helped heroes such as Perseus, Achilles and Odysseus - though her love for these figures had nothing erotic about it. Athena and Artemis had decided never to marry - even other gods - and to keep their virginity.

According to the traditional account, Poseidon and Athena quarrelled over which of them should be the patron of the city of Athens and whose name the city would bear. In the end, it was decided that each of them should make the city a gift, and the donor of the gift which the other gods

Depiction of the greatest monument of all times, the temple dedicated to the goddess Athena. A work of Iktinous, Callicratis, decorater with sculptures by the superb Pheidias.

Athena on a stele wearing a Doric veil with a helmet but barefoot. (Relief from 460 B.C., Athens, Acropolis Museum).

judged most valuable would become the patron of the city. Poseidon struck the rock of the Acropolis with his trident, and water gushed forth. Athena stamped her foot on the ground, and the world's first olive tree sprang up. The olive tree was thus sacred, and even in very early times was regarded as a symbol of peace. Since the time gods gave the victory to Athena, the city of Athens has borne her name and has enjoyed her protection. The goddess Athena stood by mankind, and helped men in their peaceful works. She taught the potters, assisted the poets and showed the women how to weave. The goddess is often referred to as "Pallas Athena": the word "Pallas" means "young maiden", and is still used in the modern language. Athena's usual rival is Ares, the belligerent god of war: even in **the Iliad,** the two deities were on different sides: Ares supported the Trojans and Athena the Greeks. And when Zeus gave his consent for the gods to intervene in the Trojan War, Athena dealt successfully with her rival Ares, striking the blow that decided the outcome of the conflict.

Generally Speaking the contribution made by Athena was with concerned of prudence, moderation and sober judgement. The Parthenon was sacred to her, and Athens honoured her with great feasts such as the Panathenaea.

Arachne was a young woman with great skill at weaving and embroidery. Everyone admired her work and frequently said she had been taught by the goddess Athena. But from arrogance she refused to accept that and challenged the goddess to a competition. Athena appeared disguised as an old woman and began to counsel her to be modest, judicious and pious to the gods. Arachne replied with curses. During the competition that followed the one weaver competed against the other but the subjects Arachne chose for her designs offended the gods. Thus she came to suffer the rage of the goddess. Her humiliation led Arachne to commit suicide. She hung herself, but to keep her from dying the goddess changed her into a spider ("arachnid") which is constantly spinning its web.

The period of Cecrops

Cecrops, the mythical king of Attica, son of Mother Earth, was a man from the waist up while the rest of his body was that of a serpent. During the time of his reign, the competition took place between Athena and Poseidon to determine who would finally take Athens (which was called Cecropia until then). Cecrops, together with Cranaus, who later succeeded him, played the role of arbiters.

Bronze statue of the goddess Athena from Piraeus. (Circa 340-330 B.C., Athens, Archaeological Museum).

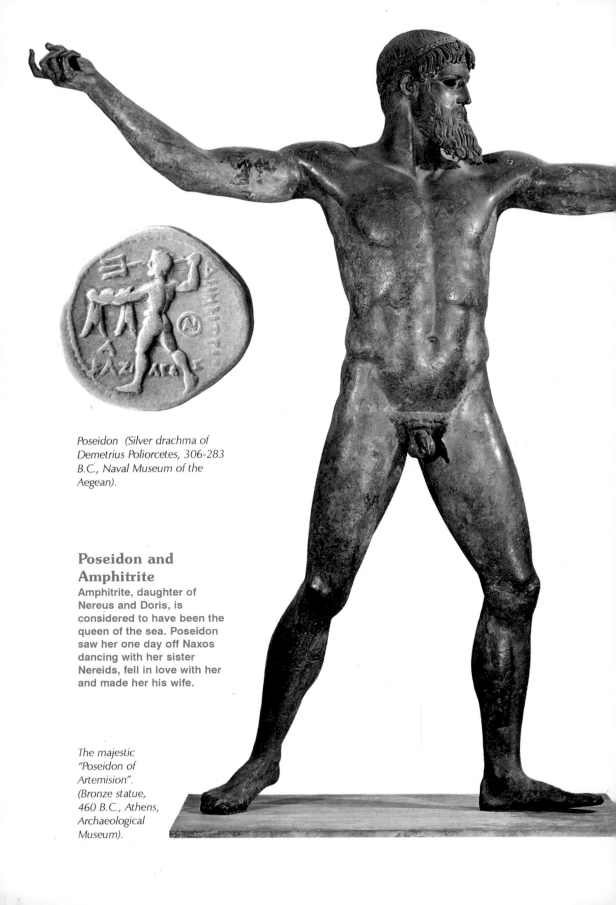

Poseidon (Silver drachma of
Demetrius Poliorcetes, 306-283
B.C., Naval Museum of the
Aegean).

Poseidon and Amphitrite

Amphitrite, daughter of
Nereus and Doris, is
considered to have been the
queen of the sea. Poseidon
saw her one day off Naxos
dancing with her sister
Nereids, fell in love with her
and made her his wife.

The majestic
"Poseidon of
Artemision".
(Bronze statue,
460 B.C., Athens,
Archaeological
Museum).

POSEIDON, god of the sea

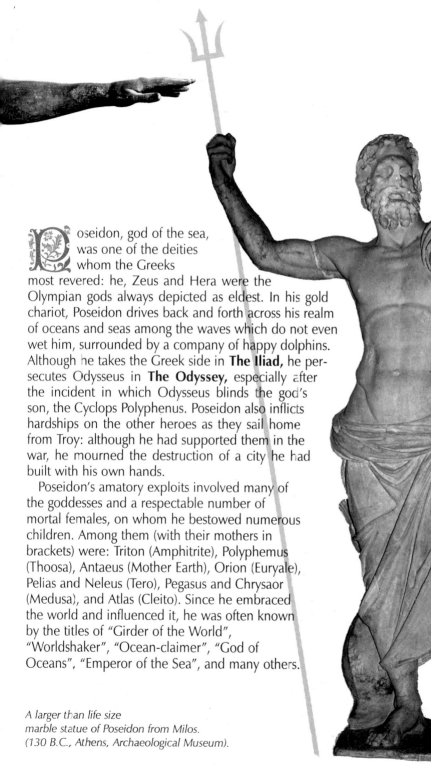

Poseidon, god of the sea, was one of the deities whom the Greeks most revered: he, Zeus and Hera were the Olympian gods always depicted as eldest. In his gold chariot, Poseidon drives back and forth across his realm of oceans and seas among the waves which do not even wet him, surrounded by a company of happy dolphins. Although he takes the Greek side in **The Iliad,** he persecutes Odysseus in **The Odyssey,** especially after the incident in which Odysseus blinds the god's son, the Cyclops Polyphenus. Poseidon also inflicts hardships on the other heroes as they sail home from Troy: although he had supported them in the war, he mourned the destruction of a city he had built with his own hands.

Poseidon's amatory exploits involved many of the goddesses and a respectable number of mortal females, on whom he bestowed numerous children. Among them (with their mothers in brackets) were: Triton (Amphitrite), Polyphemus (Thoosa), Antaeus (Mother Earth), Orion (Euryale), Pelias and Neleus (Tero), Pegasus and Chrysaor (Medusa), and Atlas (Cleito). Since he embraced the world and influenced it, he was often known by the titles of "Girder of the World", "Worldshaker", "Ocean-claimer", "God of Oceans", "Emperor of the Sea", and many others.

A larger than life size
marble statue of Poseidon from Milos.
(130 B.C., Athens, Archaeological Museum).

DEMETER, the goddess of agriculture

emeter was the goddess of fertility, a mother-deity associated with the earth who protected cultivated soil, wheat in particular. She was also the goddess of the birth of the world: all the flowers, fruits and other living things were the gifts of Demeter. Demeter is closely linked with her daughter Persephone, whose father was Zeus, and the two female deities are usually mentioned together.

The Abduction of Persephone

ersephone, Demeter's only daughter, grew up to be a happy child in the company of her mother and the other goddesses, until one day Pluto fell in love with her and abducted her. Persephone was picking lilies in a field, when suddenly the earth opened beneath her feet and Pluto carried her off to the underworld. When Demeter discovered that her daughter was missing, she began to search for her. She wandered anxiously and sadly, day and night, across the entire known world. But no one could tell her anything. When Helios, the sun, eventually revealed the truth to her, Demeter was so angry that she left her post and duties on Olympus and, changed into an old woman, entered the service of Celeus, king of Eleusis.

The goddess Demeter, during her stay at Eleusis where she revealed her true identity, taught Triptolemus, son of King Celeus, the cultivation of wheat and set him to speading agriculture throughout the world. Demeter's symbols were ears of corn, the narcissus and the poppy, while the crane was her favoured bird.

The god of Hades scattering seeds in the field that had already been ploughed by Demeter. According to one account the god of the underworld had to accept the seed to insure a good harvest. (Red-figured pelike, 430-420 B.C., Athens, Archaeological Museum).

Before leaving Eleusis, Demeter taught its kings to honour her. The ceremonies connected to the Eleusian Mysteries were only taken part in by the initiates and they kept their secret from the rest of the world. But those who managed to become initiates had a better fate when they went to Hades.

Demeter in a symbolic initiation of Triptolemus, giving him the golden ears of corn with the exhortation to spread th practice of agriculture. At their side is Persephone with a lighted torch. (440-430 B.C., Athens, Archaeological Museum).

While she was absent in Eleusis, the earth was barren, the crops withered, no plant blossomed or bore fruit and mankind suffered from starvation. It was then that Zeus ordered Pluto to sent Persephone home, since Demeter was threatening to prevent the earth from bearing even a single stalk of wheat. Pluto agreed to send his wife back to her mother in the upper world - but before doing so, he cunningly made her eat a pomegranate seed, which was enough to bind her to the underworld for ever. And so a contract had to be made with Pluto: for eight months of the year Persephone would live in the upper world, with her mother, and for four she would stay in Hades, with her husband. Demeter agreed to this, and before long the fields were full of wheat, the trees were in leaf, the earth was carpeted with flowers and all the plants were heavy with fruit. Since then, everything has been green and fertile for eight months of the year. But for the four months when Demeter loses her daughter, it is as if nature has died.

35

APOLLO or Phoebus the god of light, music and prophecy.

As the children of Zeus and Leto, Apollo and his sister belonged to the second generation of Olympian gods. Pursued by Hera, the pregnant Leto searched desperately for somewhere to give birth to her children. In fear of the queen of the gods, all the Greek cities drove her away. In the end, the barren islet of Delos - then called Ortygia - gave her sanctuary, and it was there that Apollo and Artemis were born. As soon as the god of the sun, of prophecy and of music saw the light of day, the island began to glow and the whole world shone.

As Apollo grew, he performed astounding feats, including ridding Delphi of the dragon Pytho, whom he killed with his arrows. As a result, he was called Pythian Apollo, the Pythian Games took their name and the priestess of the oracle became known as the Pythia. The Pythia squatted on the sacred tripod of Apollo inside the god's oracle, and made prophecies. The paean, a hymn in honour to Apollo, was first sung to mark this great victory and his possession of the oracle, which had previously belonged to Thetis.

Apollo was a handsome god: tall and well-made, he had

Apollo with his lyre (Athens Academy).

Apollo executing a libation. (Interior of a cylix, 490 B.C., Delphi, Archeological Museum).

Statue of Apollo from the west frieze of the temple of Zeus at Olympia. (457 B.C., Olympia, Archaeological Museum).

flowing locks and enjoyed frequent romantic encounters with nymphs and mortal maidens. Once he fell in love with Daphne, daughter of the river-god Peneus. She, however, did not return his affections, and when Apollo was chasing her one day she begged her father to transform her in order to save her virtue. No sooner said that done; the nymph became the bay-tree, which in Greek bears her name and which is sacred to Apollo.

Apollo's involvements with these nymphs and beautiful girls made him the father of many children (again, their mothers in brackets): Orpheus (Calliope), Asclepius (Coronis), Linus (Psamathe), Aristaeus (Cyrene), Troilus (Cassandra), and others. In addition, Apollo had a weakness for handsome youths such as Hyacinthus and Cyparissus, whose deaths took the form of a transformation into a flower, in one case, and a tree in the other, to the great grief of Apollo.

Apart from his achievements in music, the pastroral arts and prophecy, Apollo was also a god of war, with particular skill in shooting arrows over great distances. Mankind paid him the highest honours, dedicating to him sanctuaries, oracles, athletic contests and sacrifices. He was a religious symbol in art and the cults, and according to some accounts was the father of Pythagoras.

Hymen was the son of Apollo who married one of the Muses. He was the personification of the wedding song which was sung during the preparation of the bride, a hymn of farewell to her female virginity.

ARTEMIS, goddess of the moon and the hunt

The famous temple at Ephesus, which was considered one of the seven wonders of the ancient world, was dedciated to Artemis. It was 109 meters long and 55 meters wife. Tradition says that the Praxiteles did the magnificent altar while the peribola of the temple was decorated with statues by Pheidias, Myronas, Polycleitis and painted works by Apelles.

Artemis, the daughter of Zeus, was born to Leto on the same day as her brother Apollo. She was the goddess of the hunt, and of the moon. When she was a girl, she begged Zeus to allow her to remain unmarried and so she roamed the forests, girt with her bow and arrow and accompanied by deer and her beloved wild beasts. Artemis took part in the Battle of the Giants, where with the help of Heracles she killed the Giant Gration.

She was a vengeful deity, punishing all those who showed her disrespect. She protected hunters and the innocent. One well-known story is that of the revenge that she and Apollo took on Niobe, daughter of Tantalus. Niobe boasted that she had given birth to fourteen children, while Leto had only two. The two gods avenged this slight on their mother by shooting Niobe's children dead with their arrows, Apollo the boys and Artemis the girls.

Another victim of the goddess' vengeful rage was Actaeon, son of Aristaeus and the Nymph Cyrene who had learned the art of hunting from the Centaur Chiron. The goddess Artemis was furious with him because he had once seen her bathing naked in a pool. The goddess took cruel revenge. She transformed him into a stag and then set his own fifty dogs on him who tore him to pieces.

In the photographs on this page are four statues depicting Artemis. Two of them have the spare appearance of the "huntress" goddess, while the other two depict the goddess dressed in an elaborately ornamented costume. Impressive are the breast-like protrubances on her torso, symbolic of fertility.

Artemis was usually
honoured in mountainous
and wooded places, and she
had a famous temple at
Ephesus. She was the
patron of the Amazons, a
tribe of women who lived
apart from men and paid her
special honour.

*Bronze statue of the goddess
Artemis. (Around the middle of
the 4th century B.C., Piraeus
Museum).*

Hermes taking the new-born Dionysus to the Nymphs. (Detail from a white calyx krater, circa 440 B.C., The Vatican).

Hermaphrodite was the gorgeous son of Hermes and Aphrodite who travelled throughout the world. But a Nymph fell so deeply in love with him that in the midst of a passionate embrace she pleaded with the gods to never separate their bodies. The gods listened to the plea of the Nymph and created a new being with a double nature.

On the opposite page: the famous statute by Praxiteles. Hermes and the new born Dionysos (330 B.C., Olympia, Archaeological Museum).

HERMES, the god of commerce and prophecy, the messenger of the gods and bearer of dead souls.

Hermes was the son of Zeus and Maia, a beautiful girl who was one of the Pleiads. Even as a baby it was clear that he was going to be crafty beyond compare and a sly god. While still in swaddling-clothes, he stole the oxen of his half-brother Apollo and hid them so well that Apollo needed all his oracular talents and techniques to find them. In fact, he he might never have found them at all without the help of Zeus, fair-minded as ever. The incident passed without rancour and the half-brothers were reconciled when Hermes presented Apollo with a lyre he had himself invented and made out of the shell of a tortoise.

Apollo, in return, made him a gift of the oxen and taught him divination. Hermes was the god of commerce and

Dedicatory relief which depicts Hermes leading the chariot of Echelus with the Nymph Basile. (Circa 410 B.C.).

theft, and he served as the herald of the gods. There were wings on his helmet and his heels, and he bore a sceptre. Apart from his task of taking messages wherever Zeus sent him, he was also entrusted with the task of escorting the souls of those who died to Hades. In the myths, we often find him helping the heroes - Heracles, Perseus and Odysseus - in a myriad of ways. When Hera turned Io into a cow, Hermes released her by killing her guard-dog Argos; henceforth he was known as "the Argos killer".

Hermes was the father of many children. Among them (their mothers in brackets) were: Myrtilus (Clymene), Polyvus (Chthonophile) and Autolycus, the grandfather of Odysseus (Philonis). Pan, Arpalycus, Abderus and others were also believed to be his sons.

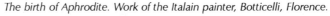

APHRODITE, the goddess of beauty and love

There are two different myths about the birth of Aphrodite, goddess of love and beauty. One we have already mentioned: that she was the daughter of Zeus and Dione. The other relates that she sprang from the seed of Uranus when his genitals fell into the sea after his mutilation by Cronus. As a result, she "emerged" from the foam as Aphrodite Anadyomene; Zephyr blew her to Cythera and then to the coast of Cyprus, where she stood on dry land.

Aphrodite was the patron of love and lovers, and her favourite pastime was causing the gods to fall in love with mortal women. She enjoyed weaving plots and enmeshing the gods in love affairs - especially Zeus, whom we find embroiled in various intrigues at different times.

Nor was Aphrodite herself to be left out of the game. Although married to the lame god Hephaestus, she embarked on an affair with Ares. In **The Iliad,** Homer tells us the scandalous tale: Hephaestus found out about Aphrodite's goings on from Helios, the sun god who saw everything, and decided to lay a trap for her and Ares. He made a magic net which was very complex and pretended

On the opposite page: the god Pan endeavoring to embrace the naked Aphrodite who is threatening him with her sandal. A smiling Eros between them. (100 B.C., Athens, Archaeological Museum).

The birth of Aphrodite. Work of the Italain painter, Botticelli, Florence.

to set off for Lemnos. That night, when Ares came to Aphrodite's bed for their assignation, Hephaestus caught them in his net and immobilised them just at the crucial moment. He then called on Zeus and the other gods to make his complaint. The goddesses, in shame, refused to attend, but the gods went with enthusiasm. Apollo laughingly remarked to Hermes that although Hephaestus was lame he had done well to catch the lovers in the act and embarrass Ares before the other gods. "How would you like to look such a fool?" he asked him. Hermes, cunning as ever, replied

Aphrodite emerging from a shell.
(Clay statuette, Athens, Archeological Museum).

that he envied Ares the chance of bedding Aphrodite, and that he himself would have been prepared to be bound three times in chains and exposed to the view of the goddesses as well as the gods. And so the incident ended in general laughter from the gods, or so Homer tells us.

Her union with Ares brought Aphrodite the four children we have already mentioned: Eros, Deimus, Phobus and Harmony.

Ares was far from being Aphrodite's only lover. The others included the handsome Adonis and also Anchyses, to whom she bore Aeneas: when Troy fell, Aphrodite saved her son and helped him to flee his family.

Aphrodite was particularly fond of roses and myrtle, and her chariot was drawn by two doves, her favourite bird.

The Venus de Milo (end of the 2nd c. B.C., Paris, Louvre).

ARES, the god of War

Ares, the fierce god of war, is always shown in armour and wearing a helmet, ready for battle. Wherever war and bloodshed broke out, wherever there was combat, Ares was to be found. As a result, he was rarely worshipped and we know of no cities where he was patron. The son of Zeus and Hera, he often fought with the other gods - even with his own father. He was worshipped at Thebes, where he was believed to be the forefather of the royal dynasty, since Harmony, wife of king Cadmus of Thebes, was his daughter by Aphrodite. The myth of the union between the fearful god of war and the tender, loving Aphrodite was a well-known one, which was also said to have produced Eros, Phobus ("fear") and Deimus ("terror"). Ares was the father of other children, too: Cycnus, Diomedes of Thrace (the owner of man-eating horses), Lycaon, Meleager, Dryas and Oenomaos.

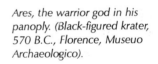

Ares, the warrior god in his panoply. (Black-figured krater, 570 B.C., Florence, Museuo Archaeologico).

Ares displayed a great preference for the area of Thrace. It is thought he dwelt in that wild area which had many horses and was a place that warrior nations often passed through. It has even been suggested that the war-loving Amazons, the daughters of the god Ares, lived there.

Castor, Ares and Pollux (or, according to others, Poseidon, Ares and Hermes) clash with four Giants on high. (Red-figured pelike from 400-300 B.C., Athens, Archaeological Museum).

45

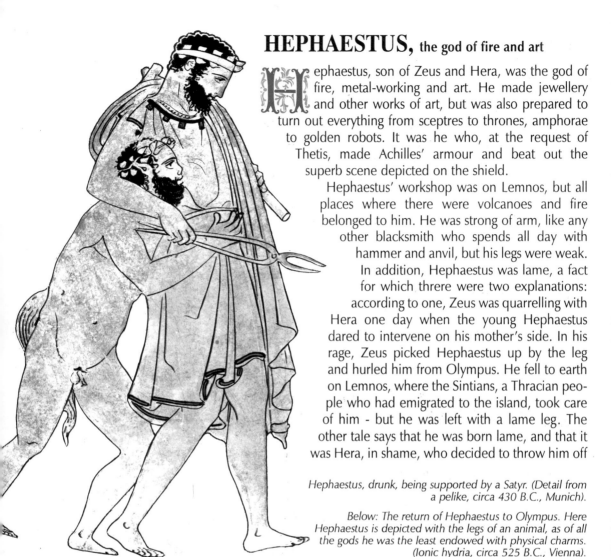

HEPHAESTUS, the god of fire and art

ephaestus, son of Zeus and Hera, was the god of fire, metal-working and art. He made jewellery and other works of art, but was also prepared to turn out everything from sceptres to thrones, amphorae to golden robots. It was he who, at the request of Thetis, made Achilles' armour and beat out the superb scene depicted on the shield.

Hephaestus' workshop was on Lemnos, but all places where there were volcanoes and fire belonged to him. He was strong of arm, like any other blacksmith who spends all day with hammer and anvil, but his legs were weak. In addition, Hephaestus was lame, a fact for which threre were two explanations: according to one, Zeus was quarrelling with Hera one day when the young Hephaestus dared to intervene on his mother's side. In his rage, Zeus picked Hephaestus up by the leg and hurled him from Olympus. He fell to earth on Lemnos, where the Sintians, a Thracian people who had emigrated to the island, took care of him - but he was left with a lame leg. The other tale says that he was born lame, and that it was Hera, in shame, who decided to throw him off

Hephaestus, drunk, being supported by a Satyr. (Detail from a pelike, circa 430 B.C., Munich).

Below: The return of Hephaestus to Olympus. Here Hephaestus is depicted with the legs of an animal, as of all the gods he was the least endowed with physical charms. (Ionic hydria, circa 525 B.C., Vienna).

Olympus. He fell into the Ocean, where Tethys and Eurynome saved him and brought him up in a sea cave. Hephaestus had his revenge on his mother, though. When he grew up he sent her a golden throne he had made. As soon as Hera sat down on it, she found herself bound to her seat and no one but Hephaestus could release her. All the pleas and wiles of the other gods were needed to tempt Hephaestus back to Olympus to set Hera free. It is said that Zeus decided to square matters with Hephaestus by giving him Aphrodite as his wife. Although Hephaestus was extremely ugly, we always find him in the company of beautiful women, including Chare (beauty personified) and Aglaea, the youngest of the three Graces.

Among the sons of Hephaestus were Palaemon the Argonaut, Arbalus the sculptor, Periphetes the robber (who was killed by Theseus) and Erithonius.

HESTIA, the goddess of family peace

As her name ("hearth") indicates, Hestia was the personification of the family home. The eldest daughter of Cronus and Rhea, Hestia asked her brother Zeus to let her remain a virgin, despite the fact that both Poseidon and Apollo wanted her for a wife. The serenity of Hestia's life on Olympus and the stability of her position there meant that she played little part in events and her presence is confined largely to the world of ideas.

In this representation Hestia, the goddess of family peace, is depicted holding a branch with fruit while Ganymede, protected by Zeus, fills his glass with wine.

THE LESSER GODS

Besides the twelve Olympian gods there were other gods who were also frequently worshipped, the difference being their seat was not on Olympus or they were the child of a god and a mortal, such as Asclepius. The worship of these gods is of great interest because it is often identified with the way of life, the religious ceremonies and the civilization of a given period.

The god Dionysus on a tiger he has tamed himself (Mosaic depiction).

The Satyrs were demonic spirits of nature and were also called Seleni. They had a human body and the legs of a billy goat or a horse with a tail. They frequently had an animal's ears such as those of Marsyas, the best known of the Satyrs. In many depictions, the human element is predominant, even in the lower extremeties. These spirits were followers of the god Dionysus and were mentioned in the section dedciated to him.

The satyr Marsyas had the avility to play the flute with divine skill. This upset Apollo who was proud of his talent and challenged Marsyas to a competition: if he lost he would do whatever the god asked. Unfortunately for the flatist the god treated him very harshly.

Head of Dionysus (Detail from amphora, circa 530 B.C., Taraquinia).

Dionysus and Midas
Midas, the king of Phrygia, was granted the ability by Dionysus to have whatever he touched turned into gold. But since he was then not able to touch food or his beloved daughter he begged the god to free him of this gift. Following the advice of Dionysus he bathed in the Pactolus river which since then has been filled with deposits of gold.

On the oppostie page: copper krater which depicts Dionysus and Ariadne in a tender scene (350-330 B.C., Thessaloniki, Archaeological Museum).

Dionysus, *god of wine and gaiety*

emele was one of the daughters of Cadmus, king of Thebes. Zeus fell in love with her beauty, but their relationship did not escape the notice of the jealous Hera. In order to harm Semele, Hera told her that if she wished to be regarded as Zeus' wife she would have to see him in all his glory, as he had been on the day of his wedding to Hera. Although Zeus tried to dissuade her, Semele fell for Hera's deception and insisted on having this proof of love. But when Zeus gave in and appeared in her chambers mounted on his chariot amidst thunder and lightning, casting his bolts of fire, he set the palace alight and Semele died from a bolt of lightning - or perhaps he just scared her to death.

However, she had been carrying Dionysus in her womb for six months. So that the baby might not burn to death, Mother Earth quickly caused cool ivy to grow and protect him from the flames. Zeus picked up the baby - still in an embryonic state - made an opening in his thigh, and left Dionysus there until it was time for him to be born, so as to spare him the jealousy of Hera. When the day came, Zeus broke the stitches and brought his son Dionysus out into the light. As a result of these adventures, Dionysus was described as "fire-born", "thigh-sewn" and "twice-born".

But he had Hera constantly in pursuit of him. She soon found out that Zeus had given the child to Semele's sister Ino and her husband Athamas. So Zeus took him away again and turned him into a goat, after which he put the infant in the charge of Hermes, with instructions that he was to be taken far into Asia until he grew up. But the rage of Hera haunted him - to the point where it drove him mad and he wandered aimlessly. Rhea cured him, and he continued on his travels. Wherever he went, he spread the culture of the vine and the rituals associated with every stage of its cultivation. Some cities accepted him in friendship, others drove him away. In Aetolia, king Oeneas was among his warmest friends, but it was in Attica that the growing of the vine reigned supreme.

Dionysus is the god of wine, of green growing things, and of the fertility of the vineyard. The Dionysiac cult was associated with wine, dance and everything that gets mankind out of the daily rut. The Dionysiac "orgies" were organised festivals with religious rites and included holy works: the word "orgy", which is Greek, originally meant "mystery". The rituals were accompanied by the chanting of the dithyramb, the song in worship of Dionysus.

The myth of Ariadne, whom Theseus left on Naxos on his

A Maenad dancing madly with a snake in her hair, rather than a band. In her right hand she is holding a cane rod with ivy leaves and in her left a leopard. (From the interior of a cylix of 490-485 B.C., Munich, Staatlich Antikensammlungen).

Representation of a Dionysian feast where the Satyrs are playing music and the Maenads are dancing. (Detail from a hydria, 530 B.C., London).

return to Athens from Crete, is bound up with Dionysus. According to the myth, it was Dionysus who kept Ariadne on the island and made her his wife. They had children, too: sons called Staphylus and Oenopion.

The company of Dionysus was made up of Nymphs, Sileni, Satyrs and Maenads. The Sileni were men with the legs and tails of horses, who pursued the Nymhs and revelled with them in caves. The best-known of the Sileni was Marsyas, a superb flautist and teacher of music. The Satyrs, who were also demons of nature, were often identified with the Sileni because they were similar, although some sources say the Satyrs were half-man, half-goat. The Maenads, or Bacchae, were women who personified the orgiastic spirits of nature. During the Dionysian orgies they were overcome by a mania for dance, song and frenetic merry-marking. This happy company was constantly around Dionysus, creating wherever they went. As we have already seen, they even took part in the Battle of the Giants, on the side of Zeus.

Asclepius, *the god of medicine*

sclepius was a hero, and also the god of medicine. The son of Apollo by Coronis (or Arsinoe, according to others), Asclepius spent time in youth with the Centaur Chiron, as did almost all of the important men of his time. The wise Centaur taught him medicine, at which Asclepius became most proficient. In fact, he was credited with the power to raise the dead - an achievement which filled Zeus with the fear that the order of the world might be in danger of being disturbed. He cast a thunderbolt at Asclepius, killing him. Apollo avenged the death of his son by killing the Cyclopses. Asclepius' wife was Epione, and the myths give him two sons, Podaleirius and Machaon, both of them physicians, and five daughters, Aceso, Iaso, Panacea, Aegle and Hygeia. After his death Zeus set Asclepius among the stars holding a curative serpent.

Hygeia, the most important daughter of Asclepius, was the personification of psychic and bodily health. There is no

Statue of Asclepius, Roman period. (Rhodes Museum).

Votive relief on which is depicted Asclepius leaning on his staff, that is wound with a snake, his two doctor sons Podalerius and Machaon, his three daughters, Iaso, Aceso and Panacea as well as a family of supplicants. (First half of the 4th century B.C., Athens, Archaeological Museum).

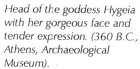

Head of the goddess Hygeia with her gorgeous face and tender expression. (360 B.C., Athens, Archaeological Museum).

specific myth related to her. She belonged to the assembly of Asclepius and was worshipped together with him.

Asclepius' art of medicine was continued by his descendants, the Asclepiads, the most famous of whom was Hippocrates.

Helios ("The Sun")

The renowned statue, "The Colossus of Rhodes", one of the seven wonders of the ancient world, was a representation of the god Helios. It was made of bronze and stood 32 meters high. The illustrious sculptur Chares from Lindos, Rhodes, took a dozen years to make it. The work cost three hundred talents and stood with its legs spread, one on each side of the entrance to the harbour; even the largest ships could pass between them. According to one myth Helios married Rhodes and therefore he was widely worshipped on the island. Fifty-six years after its erection the statue was levelled by an earthquake.

Iris between two war chariots. Drawing done by the Frenchman Nadar from a black-figured Archaic hydria.

Helios, *the god of light*

Helios, the sun god, was older than the gods of Olympus. The son of the Titan Hyperion and the Titaness Theia, he was descended from Uranus and Mother Earth. Io (the dawn) and Oceanus were his brother and sister, and he had a number of famous children: the sorceress Circe, Aetes the king of Colchis, Pasiphae the wife of Minos, and Perses.

Helios is shown as a handsome man whose golden locks are crowned with the gold rays of the sun. He is depicted driving across the sky in his fiery chariot, drawn by horses of unsurpassed speed.

The sun god above the Earth and the Ocean, in his chariot all day, using a craft like a huge, deep cup to cross the sea.

Helios sees everything, and in various myths is a witness to acts of good and evil.

The stars, like children, diving into the sea as the sun rises. (Red-figured calyx krater, 435 B.C., London).

Iris, *the messenger of the gods*

Iris was descended from the line of Oceanus, and Thaumas and Electra were her parents. She is the personification of the rainbow, a symbol of union between the sky and the earth (Uranus and Mother Earth). Iris is depicted with wings, dressed in a gauzy veil, and she serves Zeus as a messenger much as Hermes does, passing on news and the orders of the gods.

Pluto leading Persephone to his dark kingdom. Hecate is lighting the way in front and Hermes is accompanying them.
(Apulian krater, 360-350 B.C., London, British Museum).

Sisyphus, the wily son of Aeolus, was the slyest man who ever lived and did a host of cunning tricks in both this world and the other. That is why he was sentenced to the eternal punishment of pushing a huge stone up the slope of a hill only to have it roll down again, the minute he reached the top. Then the whole process had to be done over from the beginning. This myth inspired the novelist Albert Camus to write a work of the same name.

Hades (Pluto), *the god of the underworld*

Hades, the brother of Zeus, Poseidon and Hera, was the god who ruled the underworld, and he came third in the hierarchy when Creation was shared out amongst Zeus, Poseidon and himself. Hades had suffered the same fate as his siblings - that is, he had been swallowed by Cronus and then vomited out. He took part in the Battle of the Titans, on Zeus' side.

In his kingdom of darkness, Hades was harsh and ruthless. None of the inhabitants of the underworld was permitted to return to the land of the living. He had various demons and servants, such as Charon, who as ferryman took souls across the river Acheron in his boat, to the kingdom of the dead on the other side. His fee was one obol - a coin which was buried with each dead person.

Hades, as we have seen in the section on Demeter, fell in love with her beautiful daughter Persephone. Among the heroes, Heracles, Orpheus and Odysseus succeeded in descending, alive, into the underworld. Homer tells us of the darkness and despair which prevailed there, even for the most renowned of heroes.

Tantalus, king of Phrygia, was one of the most severely punished figures in Hades. He was condemned to eternal thirst and hunger. Though practically submerged in water, the moment he tried to drink the water dried up. When he stretched out his hand to pluck fruit from a branch hanging before him, the fruit vanished. This was because the gods were punishing him for being overbearing: he revealed divine secrets to mortals and stole ambrosia and nectar to offer to his mortal friends. Another version says that in order to ingratiate himself with the gods he slaughtered his son, cooked him and offered him up as a meal to these same gods.

Pan, *the god of forests and bucolic life*

Pan, an elemental figure in Greek nature, was the god of shepherds and herds. Even in the earliest times he is depicted as a kind of demon, half-man, half-goat, with a weather-beaten face, a pointed chin, a beard, horns on his forehead and a hairy body. Agile in his moments and cheerful, Pan embodied the bucolic life lived by cool springs and in shady woods. He was a highly sexual fellow and engaged in erotic games with Nymphs or young boys. Pan spent his time grazing his flocks and playing his pan-pipes, an instrument which he - as we can see from the name - is supposed to have invented.

Pan's background is far from clear. He was born in Arcadia, and may have been the son of (Cronus with Rhea) or Hermes. According to one myth, when the Nymph who was his mother gave birth to him and saw what a monster she had brought into the world, she abandoned him. But Hermes found him, wrapped him in the skin of a hare and took him to Olympus. The gods found him appealing, and allowed him to stay with them. He was a particular favourite of Dionysus, who took him travelling.

Pan fell in love with many of the Nymphs but was often rejected - as was the case with Peuce, who turned herself into a pine-tree to elude him.

He loved the beautiful Echo, the Nymph of springs and forests, but when she did not return his love he dismembe-

Statue depicting the god Pan, standing, with the feet of a goat. (Athens, Archaeological Museum).

The god Pan, sitting cross-legged playing his pipe as three Nymphs dance. (Athens, Archaeological Museum).

bered her. It is said Echo loved Narcissus hopelessly and died of grief leaving only her voice behind. Pan greatest success in these escapades was with *Selene* whom he deceived by turning himself into a sheep.

Priapus, *a fertility god*

Priapus looked rather like Pan. The sources call him the son of Dionysus by the Nymph Chione, or of Dionysus and Aphrodite, or Hermes, or even of Zeus. He grew up in Lampsacus, which he was reputed to have founded. Priapus was the god of fertility - in the plant world as well as in the animal kingdom - and of physical love.

The excessively large penis of Priapus, ever at the ready for reproduction (and for punishment), was intended to impose his will on those whom he protected and controlled. According to another view, this feauture was a projection and representation of the male organ as the bringer of life and creation.

Statuette of the god Pan sitting on a rock, (Hellenistic period, Athens, Archaeological Museum).

Eros, *the son of Aphrodite*

The naked boy with gold wings on his shoulders, curly hair and the bow from which he shoots his magic arrows, was for the ancient Greeks the son of Aphrodite and Ares long before he became the darling of the poets, painters and sculptors. The wounder of the hearts of gods and men was regarded as the most beautiful of the gods because he inspired in them the finest feeling and helped to unite couples. Right from the beginning, Eros could soften the hardest heart and the roughest character among men, bringing beauty and meaning to life.

A relief depiction showing the repeated figure of Eros.

Themis, *the goddess of justice*

Themis, the goddess of justice, looked after moral order among gods and men. She protected the weak and ill - treated. Themis possessed the gift of divination, and had her own oracle at Delphi before it was taken over by Apollo, to whom she passed on her oracular skills. Themis was he daughter of Uranus and Mother Earth, and the sister of Cronus, Rhea, Mnemosyne, Oceanus and the other Titans.

Her union with Zeus produced the Hores ("hours"), Eunomia ("order of law"), Dice ("justice") and Eirene ("peace"), who looked after the works of men, along with the three Fates. The first of the three Fates, Clotho, spun the thread of human life; the second, Lachese, shared out joy and sorrow, and the third, Atropos, cut the thread to bring life to an end.

The Erinnyes

When Cronus mutilated the Sky, castrating him with a sickle, the blood that dripped to Earth gave birth to the Erinnyes: Ellecto, Tisiphone and Megaera. Cruel, implacable goddesses, they exercised control over conscience and persecuted every transgression. Sometimes they inflicted punishment in the personification of remorse after an unjust act and sometimes like terrible figures with a death-like mien, they hunted down and punished all hideous crimes and incest.

They came to people's dreams, disturbed their sleep and there was no place on earth where one could hide from them. The unjust could hear their voices admonishing them and reminding them of how impious and indecent they were, giving them no peace day or night.

The Erinyes were a form of "divine justice" who above and beyond the justice meted out by Zeus, punished all those who transgressed the rules of ethics.

The Horae ("The Hours")

The Horae were originally seasonal divinities and only later became the personification of the hours of the day. Daughters of Zeus and Thetis, the three of them had names which represented the corresponding divinely inspired concepts: Eunomia ("good law"), Dice ("justice") and Eirene ("peace").

Sea Divinities

The sea had its own ruling spirits which belonged to the Kingdom of Poseidon.

Proteus was the patron of sea creatures and is mentioned in many myths. In **The Odyssey** he is encountered as the god of the sea who nurtures the marine animals of his liquid kingdom while Herodotus refers to him as the king of Egypt.

Triton, the son of Poseidon and Amphitrite, was half man and half fish and his sisters were the Nereids. In many depictions a host of marine divinities can be seen with the form of Triton. These Tritons attended the chariot of Poseidon or were arranged around his marine throne.

Glaucus, a sea god who was originally a man, was later transformed into a sea spirit. His form was human while his torso was covered with shells and seaweed.

There is no specific myth about **Hecate** though she is considered to be earlier than the Olympian gods and her worship through ceremonies and dedications was very widespread. According to Hesiod she was the daughter of Perses and Asteria and acted like an independent goddess. Zeus respected her and human beings sought many goods, both moral and material, from her. The main characteristic of this goddess as she evolved was her being conceived as the deity of magic, connecting her to the world of ghosts and the occult. Her places of worship were crossways which have always been considered magical sites. Her statues were erected there and the faithful left their gifts.

Triton.

OTHER LESSER GODS

p to this point we have presented only the most important gods. But besides thoese there are other lesser ones which must not be omitted or otherwise our picture of ancient Greek religion will not be as complete as it should be. These gods are by and large the personifications of abstract concepts.

Bronze head of Sleep. (4th century B.C., London, British Museum).

Eris, the goddess of discord. She was the daughter of Night and the sister and companion of Ares. This "disputatious" goddess was present at every quarrel or disagreement. Even when everyone tried to avoid her she still found a way to create disputes and to inflame passions and hate among gods and men. A characteristic example is the famous incident of the "apple of discord" which also proved to be the cause of the Trojan War.

The children of Eris were Ponos ("pain"), Lethe ("forgetfulness"), Limos ("famine"), Orcus ("oath"), Ate (the goddess of confusion), Machos ("battle"), Phonies ("murder") Pseudos ("lie") and all the other evils of mankind. That is, everything that sets off from discord.

Hebe. Her name means youth and is the joy and the beauty this age gives to human beings. Daughter of Zeus and Hera, she offered nectar to the gods. Heracles married her when he was received on Olympos. **Peitho** ("conviction"). Daughter of Oceanus, friend and assistant of Aphrodite, she convinced young girls to overcome their hesitations and give themselves over to love. **Tyche** ("fortune"). This was a goddess without any mythological content, being the personification of the abstract concept of luck. Ate, which means misfortune, was the personification of infatuation. The **Litai** were the daughters of Zeus who fixed up whatever evil **Ate** did. **Hubris** was the personification of arrogance. **Nemesis** was the goddess who brought rest to gods and people, granting them forgetfulness and relaxation. **Thanatos** ("death"), the brother of Sleep, was a figure that was confused with Hadas, Charon, and Hermes the bearer of dead souls. Sisyphus was the only one who managed to outwit death. **Anagi** ("need") was the personfications of the forces which made the decisions of Fate imperative. She was considered a wise goddess and according to the Orphic Theogony she and her sister Adrasteia were the nurses of Zeus. For the tragedians she was the supreme force to whom even the gods were obedient. **Iacchus** was the

Thanatos and Sisyphus

Once when Zeus sent Thanatos ("Death") to take Sisyphus, the latter reacted by fettering him in chains so that for a period no one died. When Zeus freed Thanatos, Sisyphus again behaved very slyly. He persuaded his wife not to inter him in the traditional way. When he reached Hades, the Lord of the Dead asked him why he was there without a proper funeral. Sisyphus then denounced his wife for disrespect and asked for permission to return to life to bring her to her senses. Thus he lived on to a great old age. But when he at last was truly dead, Hades severely punished him.

god who directed the ceremony of initiation into the Eleusian Mysteries. His name is derived from the cry of the faithful there, ("Iacche"), during the ceremony. Others consider him related to Dionysus (Bacchus) while still others believe he was the son of the goddess Demeter.

THE ORACLES

Man's natural incapacity to understand divine matters is as old as the world itself. The power of the gods brought fear, and with it hope. It was that concept which made man want to maintain contact with the divine world, to communicate with it and so to regulate his behaviour and deeds in accordance with the wishes of the gods. Even in early times, that communication took the form of oracles and oracular cults. As a result, individuals or even entire cities fell in line with the god's wishes, begging his help in taking important decisions or solving difficult problems. The divination - that is, the reliable opinion delivered by the oracle to which the faithful had addressed themselves - expressed the will of the god and determined the fate and the behaviour of the people of the time.

The most notable oracles in ancient Greece were those of Zeus at Dodona and of Apollo at Delphi. At Dodona, the priests interpreted the wishes of the god in the rustling of the leaves of the sacred oak tree, or in the cries of the doves which perched on the holy tree. At Delphi, there was a chasm in the ground; those who sat by it were overcome by inspiration. There was also the sacred Castalian spring, which was seen as prophetic, and sacred bay trees grew all around. The Pythia, priestess of the oracle, sat on a sacred tripod near the chasm in the ground, chewing bay leaves and drinking water from the sacred spring which put her in a state of ecstasy. Then the divination emerged from her mouth; this was the god's wish or his answer to the question which the supplicant had put. Envoys from kings and princes, priests and ordinary people came to Delphi every day with gifts for the god and animals to sacrifice. The oracles were usually vaguely-worded, and the question of interpreting them often arose. Supplicants would turn to the priests or soothsayers for this. Among the greatest soothsayers of antiquity were *Tiresias* and *Calchas*. We can see the power of the oracles in almost all the myths, where they often determine the lives of the heroes and the course of important events.

The prophets

Tiresias, the blind soothsayer, was one of the most important prophets of those times. We encounter him in the Oedipal myth and the Theban cycle in general. There is the following myth concerning his blinding: once when he was young and walking on a mountain he came upon two mating snakes. Tiresias pestered them (he separated them, or wounded them according to another account) and after doing that was punished and turned into a woman. Seven years later, he saw snakes mating again. He repeated his previous actions and was returned to his original sex. Once when Zeus and Hera were having a dispute over who got the most pleasure from sex, they thought of asking Tiresias, who had lived as both a man and a woman. He then replied that if pleasure had ten levels, women reached the ninth while men only achieved the first. Hera was enraged that Tiresias had revealed the secrets of her sex and blinded him. But Zeus then granted him the power of prophecy and longevity.

Calchas was a seer who was extremely adept at interpreting bird flight and knew the past, the present and the future in great detail. Apollo had given him the power of prophecy. Calchas was the prophet who followed the Achaeans to the Trojan War.

3

THE HEROES

HEROES - THESEUS - VOYAGE OF THE ARGONAUTS - PERSEUS - BELLEROPHON - DAEDALUS AND ICARUS - PHAETHON - ORPHEUS - LABDACIDS - PELOPIDS

During those ancient times mankind went through some difficult moments. The dangers of the far-off period were manifold: invincible monsters, terrible villains who ravaged a region and made it uninhabitable, horrible diseases and hideous creatures with human characteristics who were immortal by their divine nature.

Heracles and Triton.

Then the gods sent to earth their heroes, most of whom were demi-gods. Demigods were those born of a god and a mortal mother. Some were destined to become known on a panhellenic scale and others remained local heroes. The heroes were protected by the gods; they were magnificent beings and endowed with many advantages: power, virility, intelligence, magnanimity and ingenuity. Sometimes they appear as enlightened leaders who leave their throne to lead a war with a holy purpose to victory, such as Odysseus, and other times they are brave and robust young men such as Heracles, fighting to make sure that good prevails. They take on dangerous missions to fulfill a moral obligation, for the heart of a pretty princess, the acquisition of a kingdom or even the fulfillment of a divine wish. These heroes usually had a god to protect and assist them in the realization of their difficult task.

Frequently, this god rescued them from danger and punished those who were plotting against them.

Quite often the gods clashed with one another because of the heroes they had under their protection. The heroes led a very turbulent life. One could say they were predestined in this by fate and enlisted in the struggle for the good. They were glorified for their feats and acquired fame, and several of them even gained immortality.

Jason with the golden fleece in his hands, returns to lolkos where he is received by Peleus. (Apulian krater, 350-340 B.C., Paris, The Louvre). S. Page 103

HERACLES

The name of Heracles is identified with power, heroism and majesty. This demi-god, who became a symbol as his fame reached every corner of the then known world, represents a true and great super-man!

There was no "labour" that was beyond the power of Heracles. The problems which appeared in nearly all Greek societies, as well as outside it, could only be solved by one man and that was Heracles. He did battle with villains, monsters, armies, gods, natural forces, illness and was even a victor over death!

Heracles was a demi-god, endowed with supernatural gifts but also with human weaknesses. He belonged to the Perseid family and was born at Thebes, supposedly to a mortal father, Amphitryon, and Alcmene. However, his real father was Zeus, who took advantage of Amphitryon's absence one night to disguise himself as the mortal man and sleep with Alcmene.

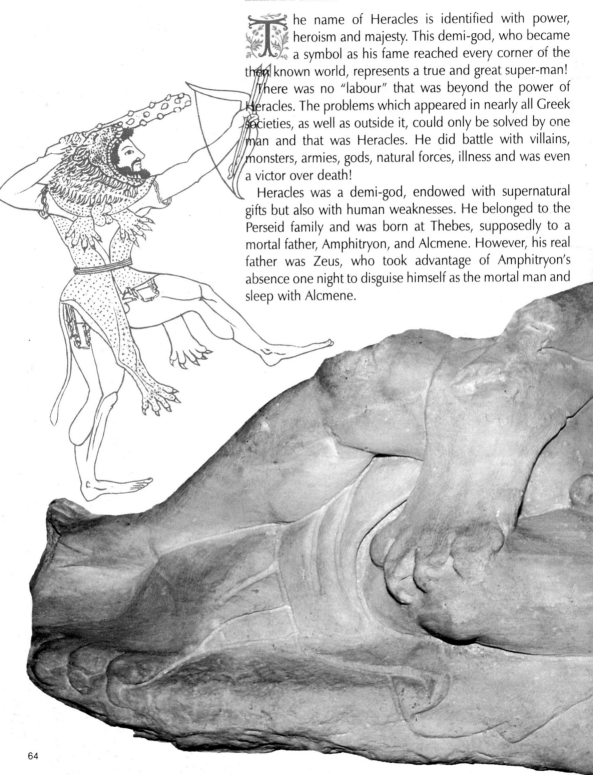

And so Heracles came to be born, with his twin brother Iphicles: he is held by the myth to be the true son of Amphitryon, since he was conceived the following evening, on his father's return.

The goddess Hera was not long in manifesting her jealousy of the infant, who was able to demonstrate his divine origins at the age of only eight months. One evening, when Alcmene had put the twins to bed, Hera sent two enormous snakes to squeeze them to death in their cradle. Iphicles began to cry, but Heracles showed no fear and seized one snake in each hand, killing them.

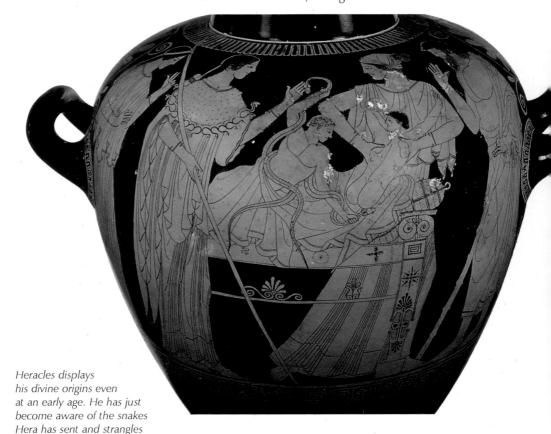

Heracles displays his divine origins even at an early age. He has just become aware of the snakes Hera has sent and strangles them boldly with the assistance of the goddess Athena. (Red-figured jug, circa 480 B.C., Paris, The Louvre).

Heracles in youth

As an adolescent, Heracles was strong, vigorous, disobedient and unusually well-developed. At eighteen, he had already accomplished his first feat, killing the lion of Cithairon which was ravaging the flocks on the mountain and which no one had been able to dispose of.

At about the same time, this tall, handsome adolescent was out walking one day when he came to a fork in the road. One branch was a fine, broad path to start with, but in the distance it could be seen to narrow. At the start of this road stood a beautiful woman in gaudy clothes. The other road was initially narrow and beset with thorns, but further along it broadened and was strewn with flowers. Here there was a woman of gentle and modest appearance, dressed simply but with nobility.

"Who are you?", Heracles asked the women.

"Come to me", said the first woman. "I will make you happy. My name is Sin".

"No, follow me", said the second. "You will gain the gratitude, respect and affection of all. My name is Virtue".

The demi-god Heracles

In the years that followed, Heracles' fame began to spread and no one could rival him in strength or bravery. Creon, king of Thebes, wed Heracles to his daughter Megara, to honour him for his bravery. But Hera was still on the lookout to harm him, and she sent Madness to overcome him. In a fit of insanity, Heracles slew the children he had had with Megara. When he recovered and realised what he had done, his first thought was suicide, but in the end he decided to seek the advice of the Delphic oracle. Pythia told him that to expiate the death of his children he would have to go to Argos and put himself in the service of his cousin, king Eurystheus, for twelve years.

On Eurystheus' instructions, Heracles was to embark on the series of labours which would grant him immortality and gain him access to Olympus. And so the popular hero presented himself before the king of Argos who, out of personal malice towards Heracles, made him risk his life in the most incredibly dangerous encounters with all the most fearsome monsters and supernatural beings he could think of.

The weaponry of Heracles included his famous club, which he made himself in order to accomplish his first labour, the sword that Hermes gave him, the bow and arrows, gifts from Apollo; Hephaestus made him a present of a gold breast-plate and Poseidon gave him horses. It is said that Athena added a veil to the breast-plate made by Hephaestus or that she herself gave him all the gifts, except for the club.

The campaign against Troy

Once Heracles led a campaign against Troy because its king Laomedon had broken his promise to reward him because he had saved his daughter Hesione from a monster who would have devoured her. He anchored in the harbour of Ilium with eighteen pentekondorous (ships with fifty oars). Along with Telemon, Heracles claimed victory. Hesione was given as a wife to Telemon and she was permitted to chose whatever captive she wished. She chose her brother Podarces who was redeemed as a slave with the veil of his sister. From then on he was called Priam from the ancient Greek verb "priamaï" which means to purchase. Priam later became the most powerful and the best known king of Troy.

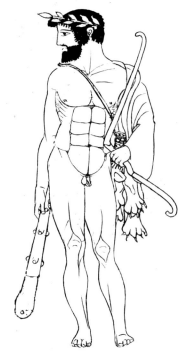

THE TWELVE LABOURS OF HERACLES

The feats of Heracles are countless and equally numberless the stories about them. But the best know are those referred to as "The Twelve Labours of Heracles" that he executed at the command of his cousin Eurystheus. Of course he performed many other feats, as we said, while organizing campaigns and waging wars as well.

Of the twelve labours, the first six took place in the Peloponnese while the other six were scattered across the globe: from Crete to Scythia, from Thrace to the end of the West and all the way to the underworld itself.

The Lion of Nemea

The first labour of Heracles was a superhuman achievement, because apart from being of supernatural size and ferocity in devouring herds and human beings, the Lion of Nemea had its lair in an inaccessible cave with two entrances. Heracles attempted to hunt the Lion down with his bow and arrow, but in vain. Then he decided to wall up one entrance to the cave and use his club to drive it inside. Once inside the cave, Heracles seized the Lion, wrestled with it and, with his superhuman strength, eventually strangled it.

Heracles skinned the Lion and wore its hide, the head of which served as a kind of helmet. It is in this lion-skin that Heracles is depicted in many paintings. As soon as Eurystheus caught sight of him wearing it, he hastened to hide, in awe of the hero's spectacular feat.

The Lion was a monster, the child of Orthrus and Echidna and the brother of another monster, the renowned Sphinx of Thebes. He had been reared by Hera (or by Selene and later ceded to Hera) who sent him to the area of Nemea where he was the cause of fear and trembling. After the labour of Heracles, Zeus placed the lion among the constellations so the hero's labour would not be forgotten.

Heracles fighting body to body with the Lion of Nemea, (Detail of a black-figured amphora, circa 510 B.C., Bresia).

The Lernaean Hydra

The Hydra of Lernaea had been wreaking havoc among the crops and flocks of the area. Even the breath emitted by its snake's heads was so poisonous that it could kill anyone standing nearby. Heracles fired burning arrows at the monster to drive it out of its lair, and as soon as it appeared he began to cut off its heads with an axe. His efforts were in vain, however, since it sprouted two heads for every one that Heracles could cut off. As the battle was going on, a huge crab which was guardian of the area bit Heracles on the leg - at Hera's instigation. Heracles was forced to kill the crab first, after which he called for the help of his nephew, Iolaus of Thebes. Iolaus set fire to a nearby forest, and as Heracles smote off the heads of the Hydra he cauterised the necks with a fiery torch so as to prevent the appearance of fresh heads. After cutting off the central head - which had been presumed to be immortal - Heracles buried it and turned it into a huge rock. The blood of the Lernaean Hydra contained a very powerful poison, and the point of any arrow dipped in it became fatal. The enormous crab belonged to the sky and, once Heracles had killed it, took the place in the zodiac appointed for it by Hera: the position of Cancer, next to the Lion (Leo).

The Hydra (water-serpent) of Lernaea was a monster born of Typhon and Echidna. It is said that Hera raised it under a plane tree at the spring of Amymone. The Hydra of Lerna is depicted as a nake-like monster which had five to one hundred heads springing from a single, amorphous body.

Heracles attacking the Lernaean hydra with an axe (Black-figured amphorae, beginning of the 5th C.BC., Paris, the Louvre).

The Hind of Ceryneia

The next labour which Eurystheus set for Heracles was to catch the hind with the golden horns which lived at Oenoe and bring it alive to Mycenae. The hind, which lived on the Arcadian mountain of Ceryneia, hid even from Artemis herself and it grazed throughout Arcadia and in the mountains sacred to the goddess above Argos. It was a unique animal, a divine creature which it was impossible to approach and very difficult to catch, even for the most skilled of hunters. Heracles hunted it for a whole year without ever getting close enough to loose an arrow. During that time, hunter and hunted passed through various countries and numerous dangers. In the end, Heracles managed to trap the animal, but on the way back he fell in with Apollo and Artemis, who were angered by his act.

Heracles apologised to the goddess and she forgave him once he had taken the beast alive to Mycenae.

The Boar of Erymanthus

The Boar was a fearsome wild beast which lived on Mt. Erymanthus, in south-west Arcadia. The animal was so crazed with anger that it destroyed the crops, and no one could approach it. Eurystheus' fourth labour was thus that Heracles should capture the animal and bear it alive to Mycenae. Heracles wandered across the

Heracles with a wild boar on his shoulder arriving at the palace of Eurysteas who runs in terror to hide in a large jar (Paris, The Louvre).

whole of Arcadia, an adventure which included his meeting with the Centaurs and his battle with them when they got drunk on the wine of Dionysus.

Heracles chased the Boar up to the snowy peak of Mt. Erymanthus, lassoed it and picked it up on his shoulders. When he arrived back at Mycenae, Eurystheus was so scared he hid in a storage jar for olive oil.

The Stymphalian Birds

These were birds which lived in a dense forest on the banks of Lake Stymphalia, in Arcadia. They were predators with wings of steel so sharp that they whistled over the heads of their enemies like knife blades.

These unusual birds of Stymphalia had become a real scourge in the area, devouring all the fruit and destroying the crops. Eurystheus ordered Heracles to exterminate them. The major problem was getting the birds out of the forest, which was too dense to hunt them in. The goddess Athena gave Heracles a set of bronze rattles made by Hephaestus, with which he was able to scare the birds and then shoot them with his arrows. Those that survived had been frightened so badly that they flew away and never troubled Lake Stymphalia again.

Heracles battling to drive off the flock of tymphalian birds. (Black-figured amphora, beginning of the 5th century B.C., Paris, The Louvre).

Heracles cleaning the Augean stables. Next to him, Athena is tranquilly observing. (Metope of temple of Zeus at Olympia, 475 B.C., Archaeological Museum).

Augeas did not believe that Heracles would be able to solve his problem. When this was done, he then broke his promise of a reward. Phyleas, son of Augeas, assisted Heracles, declaring that indeed his father had promised to reward the hero. This led to both of them being exiled by Augeas. Later Heracles returned to Elis, took revenge for the injustice that had been done him and after his victory set Phyleas up as king.

The Augean Stables

Augeas, son of Helios, was the king of Elis in the Peloponnese. He had vast herds of cattle, but had been remiss in cleaning out their stables, thus creating two huge problems for his country: on the one hand, the soil was becoming infertile because no manure was being spread on it, and on the other the accumalated filth was in danger of polluting all of Elis. Here, according to the myth, Heracles was not only acting on instructions from Eurystheus, who assigned him this labour in the hope of humiliating him with such demeaning work but Augeas, too, who had appealed to him, promising him a part of his kingdom (or one tenth of his herds) if he could complete the task in a single day. Heracles hit upon a simple but clever way of performing the work. After digging a channel into the foundations of the stables he was able to change the course of the Peneus and Alpheus rivers whose currents swept out the dung and deposited it on the farmlands of Elis. In the end, the myth goes, Augeas failed to keep his promise, and this was later the cause of war between him and Heracles. Eurystheus, too, was displeased with the hero because he had been acting for Augeas as well as for himself.

The horses of Diomedes

iomedes was a Thracian king who possessed a herd of man-eating horses nourished on the flesh of unfortunate passers by. Eurystheus dispatched Heracles to Thrace to bring the horses back to Mycenae. The hero accomplished his labour, although he had to feed Diomedes himself to the horses to do it. After eating their master, the horses calmed down and obediently followed Heracles.

One important event took place during the course of this labour. Heracles made a stop at Pherrae in order to attend the wedding of his friend Admetus to his beloved Alcestes. On precisely that day, Death had appeared in order to claim Admetus, who could be saved only if some member of his family was willing to die in his place. Of all his relatives, only Admetus' young wife was prepared to offer up her life, and so the palace of Pherrae was filled with grief and mourning when Heracles arrived. As soon as Heracles learned the news, he set out in pursuit of the funeral procession, caught up with Death and fought him hand to hand, eventually managing to save Alcestes.

Heracles among the horses of Diomides. (Bronze statuette, 3rd or 4th century B.C.)

The Cretan Bull

he Cretan Bull was a magnificent animal which emerged from the waves in response to a promise by Minos, king of Crete, that he would sacrifice to Poseidon anything that came out of the sea. But the bull was so handsome that Minos could not bring himself to sacrifice it, so he put it among his herd and sacrificed another bull in its place. Poseidon, they say, took his revenge by filling the bull with such madness that it snorted fire from its nostrils.

Eurystheus assigned Heracles the task of bringing him the bull alive. Heracles asked Minos for help, but all the king would do was allow him to capture the animal. Heracles eventually caught it alive and returned to the Argolid riding on its back as it swam. Eurystheus had planned to sacrifice the bull to Hera, but she would not accept it and so it was let free. In its wanderings it crossed the Isthmus of Corinth and ultimately reached Attica.

The Girdle of Queen Hippolyta

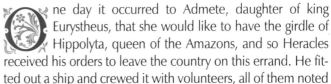

One day it occurred to Admete, daughter of king Eurystheus, that she would like to have the girdle of Hippolyta, queen of the Amazons, and so Heracles received his orders to leave the country on this errand. He fitted out a ship and crewed it with volunteers, all of them noted heroes and some of them figures as important as Theseus or Telamon, the hero of Salamis and Aegina. According to several versions, all the Argonauts sailed on this voyage with Heracles.

The Amazons were a warlike race composed entirely of women. Of the children to whom they gave birth, they allowed only the girls to live, cutting off their right breasts when they grew up so as not to obstruct their archery. They were excellent horsewomen and skilled in the arts of war, and men approached them at their peril.

Hippolyta, their queen, wore a unique belt of gold and precious stones, a gift from her father the war-god Ares, as her emblem of authority. Heracles and his heroes arrived in the country of the Amazons after an adventurous journey. Initially, Hippolyta seemed willing to give her girdle to Heracles, but Hera - disguised as an Amazon - succeeded in provoking a misunderstanding between Heracles' friends and the Amazons which ended in war. During the fighting Heracles killed Hippolyta, who believed he had betrayed her, and thus acquired the girdle. According to another version of the myth, the hostilities began as soon as the heroes landed, and the girdle was eventually handed over as ransom for Melanippe, an Amazon who may have been Hippolyta's sister and whom Heracles had captured.

The Oxen of Geryon

The demi-god's next labour was to bring to Mycenae the Oxen of Geryon, and this adventure took him to the island of Eurytheia, at the end of the West. There, the monstrous Geryon, son of Chrysaor, owned vast herds guarded by the shepherd Eurytion and the two-headed dog Orthros, littermate to other monsters such as Cerberus, the Lion of Nemea and the Lernaean Hydra. The name Geryon meant "loud-voiced", and when Geryon shouted it was as if thousands of warriors were giving tongue together. From the waist up he had three

The **Amazons** were the daughters of the god of war, Ares and the Nymph Harmony. According to some, their kingdom lay in Thrace while in the opinion of others it was in the hills of the Caucasus or even on the left bank of the Don. Outside Heracles, Bellerophon also waged war against them. The Amazons took part in the Trojan War as well, on the side of the Trojans with their incredibly beautiful queen Penthesileia. She was killed by Achilles who then fell in love with her the moment she died. The Amazons worhipped the goddess Artemis and it is said that the temple at Ephesus, which is dedicated to the goddess and was included among the seven wonders of the ancient world, was a work of the Amazons.

bodies - that is, six arms and three heads. He is also said to have had wings.

Heracles had great difficulty in reaching the end of the West, because this involved sailing across the Ocean. After much pressure and many threats, Helios agreed to lend Heracles his golden cup in which to cross the sea. As soon as he landed on Eurytheia, Heracles killed Orthros (who sprang at him) with his club and then finished off Eurytion. Then he was able to seize the valuable oxen and sail away. There are a number of tales about the feats Heracles performed during the voyage. As he sailed by, he is said to have killed various monsters and robbers who haunted the coasts of Libya and Africa. To commemorate the fact that he had been at Tartessus, he built two columns, known as the Pillars of Heracles, one on either side of what is now called the Straits of Gibraltar which separate Europe from Africa. There were lots of adventures involving the herd of oxen, too: at one point, the animals were driven mad by the biting of flies sent by Hera. In the end, some of them remained wild, but Heracles managed to get most of them back to Mycenae, where Eurystheus sacrificed them to Hera.

Heracles battling the Egyptians (Athens, Archaeological Museum).

Heracles attacking a triple-bodied monster with his sword. (Black-figured amphora, circa the middle of the 6th century B.C., Paris, The Louvre).

When Hera married Zeus,
Gaea (Earth) gave her
golden apples. The goddess
liked them to much she gave
an order to have them
planted in her garden which
lay near the Atlas mountains.
These attractive apples,
which were guarded by
nymphs and monsters, were
sought by Eurystheas from
Heracles.

The Golden Apples of the Hesperides

ar away to the west of Libya, in the foothills, perhaps, of the Atlas Mountains, was once the Garden
of the Hesperides, with its trees of golden applies.
The daughters of Atlas were forever trespassing in the garden and stealing the apples, so Hera gave the task of guarding them to an immortal dragon with a hundred heads,
assisted by the three Nymphs called the Hesperides.

On setting out on this labour, Heracles first had to find out
where the country of the Hesperides lay. Although he did all
he could to extract from the god Nereus the exact route he
should follow, he still had many adventures on the way.
One of them involved wrestling with the giant Antaeus. This
was far from easy, since as long as the giant had his feet on
the ground he could draw strength from Earth, his mother.
Heracles realised this and, with a superhuman effort, managed to lift Antaeus on to his shoulders, breaking his contact
with the ground. Then he could squeeze him in his arms in
mid-air and throttle him.

On this voyage, among other perigrinations, Hercules

*Heracles struggling with Antaeus. The latter has been immobilized on
the hero's hilt. (Red-figured krater, 510-500 B.C., Paris, The Louvre).*

Heracles and Antaeus

The giant Antaeus was the
son of Mother Earth and
Poseidon and dwelt in Libya.
Any foreigner who came to
his land was forced to fight
him. Since he was invincible
as long as he was in contact
with the Earth, his mother
from which he drew power,
he killed all the men and
dedicated the plunder to his
father Poseidon. But things
went differently with
Heracles.

freed Prometheus, the benefactor of mankind, whom Zeus
had condemned to be chained to the Caucasus Mountains
for giving mankind fire and breaking the rule which restric-
ted its use to the gods alone. Every evening, an eagle came
and tore at Prometheus' vitals, ripping out his liver, which
grew back by the following morning.

While Heracles holds the sky on his shoulders, Atlas offers him the golden apples. Further back, Athena, a faithful ally in Heracles' struggle, assists him, supporting the sky with one of her hands. (Metope of the temple of Zeus, Olympia, Archaeological Museum).

Heracles shot the eagle and released Prometheus from his chains. In gratitude, Prometheus advised Heracles not to pick the apples of the Hesperides himself, but to ask Atlas to do it for him, as a favour. The Giant Atlas was responsible for holding up the sky, on his shoulders. Heracles offered to relieve him of his burden for a while, on condition that Atlas went and picked three golden applies from the Garden of the Hesperides. Atlas fetched the apples, but was then unwilling to resume his burden, offering instead to take the precious fruit to Eurystheus. Once again, the demi-god was forced to use all his cunning: he asked Atlas to hold up the dome of the heavens for a moment while he, unused to such weights, put a cushion on his shoulders. Atlas, unsuspecting, shouldered the burden - only to discover that Heracles had snatched up the apples which Atlas had laid down and taken to his heels.

Eurystheus got his apples, but did not know what to do with them. So he gave them to Athena, who took them back to the Garden; such fruit, she knew, should not be kept anywhere but in a divine garden.

Cerberus

Cerberus, the dog of Hades, guarded the kingdom of the dead and forbade entrance to the living, though keeping the dead from leaving was his primary obligation. He had three dog heads, a snake's head for a tail any many serpent's heads reared up threateningly from his back. His father was Typhon, his mother Echidna and he is thought to have been the brother of the other monsters of this couple: the Lernaean Hydra, Orthrus, the hound Geryon and the Lion of Nemea.

This labour differs from all of Heracles' others because it involves the desecration of a sacred place and violation of the laws of nature. As the supreme feat, Eurystheus asked Heracles to bring him the guard-dog of the underworld. Only a Heracles could transcend the abilities of man so far as to be able to enter the underworld - and not only that, but to bring back its guard-dog, too. Before embarking on this adventure, Heracles was initiated into the Eleusinian Mysteries, out of respect for the lords of the underworld and for the dead. On his descent into Hades, he had the support of Athena and above all of Hermes. He entered by the route beginning in the cave by Cape Taenaron. Heracles encountered many figures he had known before, but whenever he tried to fight them and drew his sword, Hermes reminded him that he was seeing nothing but ghosts. Pluto gave his consent for Heracles to take Cerberus away with him, on condition that he could tame the animal without wea-

Heracles leading the ferocious Cerberus to Eurysteas who looks at it terror and hides in a large jar.

(Depiction on a hydria from 520 B.C., Paris, The Louvre).

pons, wearing only his breast-plate and lion-skin. So Heracles wrestled with the dog, clutching him tightly despite the wounds caused by the animal's lashing tail, until it gave in. When he took the dog back to Mycenae, Eurytheus hid in his storage jar again, out of fear, and since there seemed little else to do with Cerberus Heracles took him back to Hades where he belonged.

Heracles entering Olympus. (Black-figured cylix, 550 B.C., London, British Museum).

The death and deification of Heracles

eracles accomplished many more feats and labours during his lifetime. He served on campaigns, made war and dispatched numerous robbers and wild beasts. There are countless narratives and legends in which these doings can be found in various forms. But the hero's death is associated with his fatal marriage to Deianeira, a match which he had decided on during his descent into Hades, where he met her brother Meleager and promised to marry his sister. That agreement, made in a place like the underworld, proved to be decisive.

It so happened that when travelling together, Heracles and Deianeira had to cross the river Euenus, where the ferryman was the Centar Nessus, who lived nearby. Nessus rowed Heracles across first, and then came back for Deianeira. He attempted to ravish her - but Heracles, hearing her cries from the opposite bank, fitted an arrow to his bow and wounded the Centaur in the heart. Nessus decided to take his revenge. He told Deianeira that if she wanted to have Heracles with her for ever, should she ever be afraid of losing him, she should make a magic potion out of the blood trickling from his wound.

The Heraclids, the ancestors of Heracles, put up great struggles to maintain their rule in the Peloponnese after the deification of their demigod ancestor. One of them, **Archelaus**, the son of Temenos and the great-great grandchild of Heracles himself, driven from the area of Argos by his brothers, went to Macedonia. There he served king Cisseas, defeating the enemies who were beseiging him. After many feats and in keeping with the Oracle of Apollo, he followed a goat until it brought him to the site of Aiges. There he built the Macedonian town of Aiges, named for the goat ("aiga" in Greek). This Archelaus is thought to have been the immediate ancestor of Alexander the Great.

Heracles rushes at the Centaur Nessus who is stretching his arms out pitifully pleading for his life. (Black-figured amphora, circa 610 B.C., Athens, Archaeological Museum).

Philoctetes, the hero to whom Heracles left his bow and arrows bound himself by an oath to keep secret the place where the demi-god had died. But under pressure Philoctetes violated this oath and was punished for it. As a suitor of Helen before her marriage he too had a moral obligation to take part in the Trojan War. The great tragedians Euripides and Sophocles related the events of his life in their separate works, "Philoctetes".

The opposite page: detail from metope of the Athenian Treasure at Delphi which depicts Heracles in all his majesty at one of his labours (subduing the hind of Cerynea). (Around 500 B.C., Delphi, Archaeological Museum).

Deianeira believed him, collected some of the Centaur's blood, and took it with her.

Some time later, Heracles was victorious over Eurytus in the conquest of Oechalia. Wishing to erect an altar to Zeus and sacrifice to him, he sent his comrade Lichas to Trachis, where Deianeira was then living, to fetch him clean new clothes for the ceremony. Deianeira was afraid that the company of Iole, dauhter of Eurytus, whom Heracles had taken as his concubine, might drive his lawful wife from his mind, and so she dipped his new tunic in the blood of Nessus. Heracles put it on and began to sacrifice. But the poison in the Centaur's blood soon burned his skin. The torment was unbearable. Heracles tried to tear off the poisoned tunic, but his flesh came away with it. He ordered his companions to take him to Trachis. When Deianeira realised what she had done, she committed suicide. Heracles entrusted the care of his son Hyllus to Iole - and made Hyllus promise to marry her when he grew up - and climbed to the top of Mt Oete, where he built a bonfire and ordered his friends to set fire both to it and him. All were reluctant to obey him, and only Philoctetes had the courage to start the fire. In gratitude, Heracles gave Philoctetes his bow and the arrows soaked in th blood of the Lernaean Hydra. When the flames had begun to rise high, thunder was heard, lightning flashed and a cloud descended to take Heracles into the sky. So it came about that he joined the immortals and ascended to Olympus, where he married Hebe, the goddess of eternal youth.

THESEUS

T heseus is the hero of Athens, and he occupies a position equivalent to that of Heracles for the Dorians, although he is a generation younger. His father was Aegeus, king of Athens, and his mother was Aethra, daughter of king Pittheus of Troezen. However, in many versions his true father is Poseidon, and there are numerous myths surrounding his birth. The best-known relates how after two barren marriages Aegeus sent to the Delphic Oracle for advice. The oracle told him not to untie the mouth of his wineskin before he returned to Athens lest one day he should die of grief. Unable to understand the words of the oracle, Aegeus decided to travel home via Troezen, to consult king Pittheus, who was known for his wisdom. Whether Pittheus understood the oracle or not, he wanted his daughter to be the mother of the son whom the king of Athens wished so dearly. He arranged a great feast at which Aegeus drank deeply of the wine, after which Pittheus saw to it that he spent the night with Aethra. Waking in the morning next to the beautiful Aethra, Aegeus left her his sword and sandals, over which he rolled an enormous boulder. He left instructions that if the boy to be born was so strong that he could lift the boulder and take his father's sandals and sword, he was to be put them on and come to Athens. The sandals and sword would be the sign by which Aegeus would recognise him.

But his quest for his father had to be done with great secrecy so the Pallantids would not take notice of him and exterminate him. The Pallantids (the sons of Pallas) were the cousins of Theseus who knowing that Aegeas did not have a child, sought his throne. Theuseus was not able to avoid that threat when he arrived much later at Athens because he had to face the ambushes and the attacks of the Pallantids who wanted to usurp the throne.

Depictions that depict the feats of Theseus. In the centre the hero has already defeated the Minotaur. Right of this, toward the bottom Theseus lifts the basin against Sciron white the turfle can be seen further down. Further on below is the capture of the Marathon bull, the punischment of sines, the extermination of the pig of Phaea followed by the battle with Cercyon and finally the punishment of Procrustes. (Interior of redfigured cylix, 440-430 B.C., London, British Museuem.

The boyhood of Theseus

Theseus grew up in Troezen with his mother and grandfather, and was a strong, handsome child. There is a tale that when Theseus was seven years old Heracles visited the court of Pittheus. The hero cast aside the lion-skin he always wore when the company sat down to dinner. All the boys of the court were frightened, thinking the skin was a real lion. But Theseus picked up a club lying nearby and rushed to fight the beast, proving even as a boy how brave he was to become.

When his boyhood was over, Theseus was taken to Delphi to dedicate his shorn childish locks to Apollo, as was the custom. But he would not allow the attendants to cut off all his hair - just the curls that clustered around his forehead. This later became a fashionable way of dressing the hair that took his name: the "Theseian cut".

When he reached the age of sixteen, his mother thought he was strong enough to embark upon the next stage in his life. She revealed his paternity to him, and took him to the boulder. Theseus easily rolled it away, found his father's sandals and sword, put them on and prepared to leave for Athens. In vain Aethra and Pittheus implored him to go by sea and not by the land route, which at that time was infested with robbers and wild beasts. But Theseus, envying the glory of Heracles, was thirsty for heroic feats, and had made up his mind to travel by land.

Theseus moving the rock following the suggestion of his mother and finding the sword and sandals of Aegeas. (Clay Roman relief, 1st century A.D., London, British Museum).

The road to Athens

The first robber whom Theseus encountered, in the vicinity of Epidaurus, was called Periphetes. He lay in wait for passing travellers and killed them with a huge metal club. Theseus took his club away from him and killed him with it.

As he approached Cechreae, a second and equally dangerous opponent hove in sight. This was Sines Pityocamptes, which means "pine-bender", a son of Poseidon. Sines killed strangers in a particularly gruesome manner: he pulled down the tops of two adjacent pine trees, to each of which he tied one leg of the unfortunate traveller. Then he let the trees spring apart again, ripping his victim in two. Theseus' punishment of Sines was to put him to death in the same way.

Theseus, as he accompanies Heracles on his labour to acquire the girdle of the queen of the Amazons, Hippolyta, is bedazzled by the beauty of Antiope, whom he abducts. He had a son by her, Hippolytus. On the metope of the temple of Apollo at Eretria there is an exact depiction of the bduction of Antiope by Theseus. (510-500 B.C., Chalkida, Archaeological Museum).

Theseus captures the robber Sines with the aim of punishing him in the same way he used to torture and kill unfortunate wayfarers. (Attican cylix, beginning of the 5th century B.C., by the painter Elpinicus, Munich, Staatliche Antikensammulungen.

Theseus continued his journey and entered Corinthian territory, where he fought with spear and sword against a fearful beast of the underworld, a wild sow which belonged to an old woman called Phaea or Crommyo - a name taken from Crommyum, the place where she lived.

The next stage of his travels took Theseus into the kingdom of Megara and to the most dangerous point on his journey, the section of the road beneath the Geranian Mountains (now known as the "Bad Step"). Here the road was merely a narrow path barely wide enough for one traveller. On the one side, as the landscape still is today, were the precipitous slopes of the mountain, and on the other was a steep drop into the sea. The coastline was the haunt of a wild carnivorous turtle, which devoured all those who approached. High up on the cliffs, the pass was controlled by Sciron, a robber who made passers by wash his feet - supposedly in return for allowing them to travel on. While they were at their task, he would kick them hard down the cliff into the sea, where the turtle ate them up.

However, the gods had so arranged things that it was Sciron's fate to die in the same way. Theseus threw him down from on high, and the turtle devoured him.

Then Theseus went down to the sea and killed the turtle itself, taking its shell to make into a shield. The next kingdom he entered was Eleusis; here he had to fight the giant Cercyon, who was such a good wrestler that he had overcome all challengers. But the brave son of Aegeus overcame Cercyon, lifting him up and smashing him on the ground, where he was crushed.

One of Theseus' most renowned exploits was his punishment of the robber Procrustes, the next obstacle on his journey. This unusual robber killed his victims and took their belongings after first forcing them to lie down on his awful bed. If the poor traveller was taller than the bed was long, Procrustes cut off the extra length of leg. If, on the other hand, he was too short, the robber tied ropes to his arms and legs and stretched him till he fitted the bed. In fact, it is said that Procrustes had two beds for this purpose: a short one for tall people, and a long one for the short. Theseus dealt with him in the way he had dealt with so many.

As a result, the reputation of Theseus arrived in Athens before he did. At this time, Aegeus had just married the sorceress Medea. She knew in advance who Theseus was as he progressed towards Athens. Wihout giving away any details to the king, she managed to inspire in him a fear of the young hero, whose beauty and had already become legendary. She managed to convince Aegeus to offer Theseus a poisoned drink. But as the youth went to cut a piece off the sacrificial animal with his sword - perhaps intentionally - Aegeus recognised the weapon and then the sandals which Theseus was wearing. He sprang forward and stopped him from raising the poisoned cup, recognising as he did so his son. Aegeus poured out the contents of the cup and exiled Medea from his country.

Among the feats of Theseus in Attica was to catch the fearful bull which Heracles had brought from Crete. Some sources place this incident before Theseus' recognition by his father and some after, but however that may be the beast had been roaming the plain of Marathon destroying crops and human lives. Theseus managed to catch it, bind it with chains and sacrifice it to Apollo.

The assistance supplied by Theseus to the king of the Lapithae, Peirithous, was valuable when at his wedding the invited Centaurs got drunk and attacked the Lapithae. In this representation Theseus is punching one of the Centaurs with great gusto, who is trying to attack him with a vase while stepping on a Lapitha as he passes. (Design on a red-figured krater, 475-450 B.C., Florence, Archaeological Museum).

The Cretan Cycle

Androgeos, son of Minos, was a charismatic young man and outstanding athlete who came to Athens in order to compete in games organised by Aegeus. The young prince from Crete succeeded in beating all the other competitors. Envious of his success, Aegeus sent him against the bull of Marathon, which slew Androgeos. The news of the death of his son reached Minos as he was sacrificing on Paros. As soon as the feast was over, he summoned his fleet and sailed to attack Athens. The war lasted some time and ended with the defeat of Athens, which Minos compelled to pay him a tribute of blood: each year, seven youths and seven maidens were sent to Crete and fed to the monstrous Minotaur. The Minotaur was a monster with a human body and the head of a bull. He was the son of Pasiphae, the wife of Minos and a bull that Posiedon had sent to Minos. Minos, shamed by the birth of his monster, called on the architect Daedalus to built the Labyrinth as a palace in which the terrible Minotaur was incarcerated and fed on human bodies. Before long, Theseus had to deal with this problem when the time came to send the annual 'tribute' to Minos. The people of Athens were growing restive. It is said that Minos used to select the youths who were to be fed to the Minotaur, and to insist that they be unarmed. There was no chance of the victims surviving, since they soon got lost in the labyrinth of corridors beneath Minos' palace, where the beast lived and he devoured them at its leisure.

Theseus decided that he would be one of the seven youths sent to the Minotaur - in the hope that he could kill the beast. When the party set out for Crete, their ship had black sails, indicative of its melancholy mission. But Aegeus had given them white sails as well, which they were to hoist if they returned in joy and triumph. The white sails would signal the news of their victory even before the ship docked.

Theseus arrived in Crete, and was led to the Labyrinth with the others. But Ariadne, daughter of Minos, saw him and fell in love with him. Before the youths entered the palace, she had time to give him a ball of thread, telling him to tie one end to the entrance of the Labyrinth and unwind it as he went, so that he could find his way back.

Depiction of the labyrinth where Theseus killed the Minotaur. Roman mosaic from the 4th century A.D., Vienna.

Theseus killing the Minotaur. (Black-figured amphora, Paris, The Louvre).

She also made Theseus promise to take her back to Athens with him and marry her. Theseus killed the Minotaur with his bare fists, liberated his companions and managed to flee in secret from Crete, taking Ariadne with him. But when the ship stopped at the island of Naxos on the way back to Athens, Theseus left Ariadne there, to be consoled by the god Dionysus.

Although everything had gone well, the happy returning travellers forgot to hoist their white sails in place of the black ones. Poor king Aegeus, watching from the peak of Cape Sounion, saw the ship with its black sails, concluded that his son was dead, and threw himself to his death off the cliff into the sea which ever since has been called the Aegean.

Richard Strauss inspired by the myth of Theseus and Ariadne wrote the opera "Ariadne auf Naxos" and Maeterlinck the work "Ariadne and Bluebeard". The myth provided the stimulus for the work "Ariadne" by the French writer Pierre Corneille.

Ariadne was soon consoled by the god Dionysus. Here is a tender scene among Erotides, Satyrs and Maenads.
(Red-figured vase, circa 380, B.C., Archaeological Museum).

The arrival of Theseus' companions is depicted in a very characteristic manner in this detail of the François vase, a work of Ergotinos and Cleitias. (Circa 570 B.C., Florence, Archaeological Museum).

Marble group of Theseus and Antiope from the Temple of Apollo "Daphnephoros" ("Wreath - wearer"), Eretria, 500 - 490 B.C. Eretria, Archaeological Museum.

Sounion, on the southwest tip of Attica, is also mentioned by Homer. From here Aegeus gazed out to sea full of anticipation of the glad tidings of Theseus victory, which he did not live to enjoy. Starting in the 6th century B.C., a temple was erected at Sounion dedicated to Poseidon, the buildings of which have survived up to the present.

The kingdom and the death of Theseus

heseus proved to be a good king. He made Athens the capital of his state, established social classes, minted coins and established the Panathenaea as the festival which symbolised the political unity of Attica. He fought off the Amazons when they attacked Athens. He lived many years, married Phaedra, and accomplished numerous feats - including escaping from imprisonment in the underworld, with the help of Heracles. In his later years, he formed a close friendship with the hero Perithoos. Once, though, he went to visit his kinsman king Lycomedes of Skyros, who took him up on to a high cliff, supposedly to admire the view of the

The Temple of Athena, Sounio (Copperplate)

island to be had from there. Lycomedes treacherously pushed Theseus off the cliff and killed him.

In the historical period, it was said that the Athenian troops fighting the Persians at the battle of Marathon saw at their head a warrior hero of superhuman size. Their suspicion that this was the ghost of Theseus was confirmed by the Delphic Oracle, which told them to seek out his grave on Skyros. General Kimon, who was entrusted with the mission, identified the grave on a hill-top thanks to an eagle which was always perched on the spot. The grave yielded a coffin containing the remains of a huge man with a spear and a sword, proof of his identity. The relics were borne back to Athens and accorded a funeral worthy of this great Attic hero.

Euripides, a famous tragedian of antiquity, was perhaps referring to the son of Theseus and Hippolyta in his work Hippolytus. When Theseus' second wife Phaedra fell madly in love with "Hippolytus" but when was spurned, she reported to his father that he had attempted to rape her. In his rage Theseus beseeched Poseidon to punish his son. The god then sent an enraged bull that terrified the horses of Hippolytus; they bolted and he was thrown out and killed. Much later, Seneca was inspired by this myth as well.

THE VOYAGE OF THE ARGONAUTS

The campaign of the Greeks to Colchis under the leadership of Jason was one of the most important events of mythical times because the finest young men in Greece took part in it. But let us speak of the events that led up to this great campaign.

Phrixos and Helle

On the **Argonaut Cam** paign Ancient lyric writers, such as Pindar, were inspired by the myth of the Argonauts, but the three great tragedians also wrote works inspired by the Argonaut campaign. Aschylus presented the tragedies "Athamas", "Hypsipyle", "Argo" and "Cabiras". Sophocles took advantage of the theme in his tragedies "Athamas", "Colchids", "Skythians" and "Remotime". None of these works have survived. But the renowned "Medea" by Euripides, has survived.

Athamas, the king of Orchomenos in Boeotia, had two children by his wife Nephele: Phrixos and Helle. But Ino seduced the king and persuaded him to drive out Nephele and take her as his wife. Ino was a bad step-mother to the children. Her hate for them caused her to lay the following plan. She persuaded the women of the country to bake the seed-corn stored for the next planting. Naturally enough, the baked seed failed to sprout when planted, and so famine struck the country.

Athamas sent envoys to the Delphic Oracle to ask the god what he should do. Ino bribed the envoys to say that the oracle had told them Phrixos would have to be sacrificed to Zeus before the earth would bring forth fruit. The people rose up in anger, demanding that the king obey the oracle. Athamas had to give in, but just as Phrixos was being led to the sacrificial altar Nephele, the children's mother, sent a ram with a golden fleece.

Holding on to the horns of the ram, Phrixos flies over the sea heading for Colchis. (Red-figured pelike, circa 460 B.C., Athens, Archaeological Museum).

Phrixos and Helle mounted the ram and it flew off. As they crossed the Thracian peninsula, however, Helle looked down, became giddy and fell. She drowned in the waters of the strait known since then as the Hellespont. Phrixos arrived alone in Colchis, where the king was Aeëtes, son of Helios and Perseis and brother of the sorceress Circe. There he sacrificed the ram to Zeus, in gratitude, and begged the protection of Aeëtes, who made him his son-in-law. Phrixos, in turn, gave the king the golden fleece. Aeëtes hung the fleece on an oak tree in a grove sacred to the god Ares and set a dragon which never slept to guard it night and day.

Pelias and Jason

The king of Iolkos was Pelias, son of Poseidon and Tyro, who had usurped the throne from his half-brother Aeson. Afraid that Pelias would kill his son Jason, the rightful heir to the throne, Aeson took him to the cave of the Centaur Chiron, on Mt. Pelion, to whom he assigned the task up bringing the boy up. The wise Chiron taught Jason the learning and arts of the age, and when he was old enough set him on the road to Iolkos to claim his throne.

As the handsome young man crossed the river Anaurus, he lost one of his sandals; when he arrived in Iolkos wearing only one, king Pelias was greatly alarmed. Years before,

The Centaurs

The Centaurs were monsters, half human (from the waist up) and half horse. They had a human head, the arms and torso of a man and the four legs of a horse. Chiron and Pholus stood apart among the Centaurs because they did not have the savage character of the others. Chiron was wise and operated a school on Mt. Pelion where generation after generation of heroes studied at his side. Pholus was also good and hospitable unlike the rest of the Centaurs who were full of ill-will and passions such as Nessus whom we encountered in Heracles' adventures.

Two Centaurs are beating Peirithous, the king of the Lapithae with tree Trunks because he had gone past the limits the gods had set for mortals. (Bronze lamina, 650-635 B.C., Olympia, Archaeological Museum).

Clay figurine of a Centaur from Lefkanti, Euvoea. Arhaeological Museum

he had received an oracle that one day a man with only one sandal would come down from the mountains, take his throne and kill him.

So when Jason, his nephew, demanded the throne that was his by right, the crafty Pelias claimed that he had had a dream in which Phrixos begged him to do something to bring his spirit home, along with the golden fleece from the palace of king Aeëtes in Colchis. And so he asked the young Jason to do as this oracular pronouncement required: to build a ship and set out. In other words, Jason was to undertake the task of putting the soul of Phrixos to rest. Pelias promised and swore in the name of the gods that as soon as Jason returned with the golden fleece to Iolkos he would surrender the throne to him.

Preparations for the journey

Jason agreed to Pelias' terms and began to prepare for the voyage. He commissioned the architect and shipbuilder Argos to build him a vessel with fifty oars. Once finished, the ship was far superior to any other of its time. Thanks to a piece of wood from the sacred oak tree of Dodona which the goddess Athena had given Jason, the ship could talk and make prophecies. It was also very speedy, which was why it was called Argo ('argos' = quick).

While the Argo was being made ready, Chiron advised Jason to have heralds travel throughout Greece spreading the word of his long journey and inviting brave and noble youths to take part in the campaign. And so Jason did: and the crew of his ship, the Argonauts as they were called, were all heroes or even the sons of gods. They included *Tiphes* (helmsman of the Argo), *Orpheus* the musician, the soothsayers *Idmon* and *Mopsus, Heracles, Hylas, Idas, Castor* and *Pollux, Periclymenus* (son of Neleus), *Peleas* and his brother *Telamon*, and many others who made up the flower of the young generation of the day.

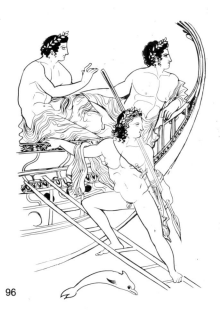

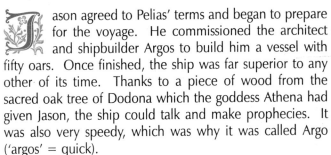

Design showing the Argonauts sitting in and around the Argo.

Depiction of the Argonaut campaign on a clay relief Roman plaque. The goddess Athena is supervising the construction of the Argo and helping the crafts man to set its mast in place (1st half of the 1st century A.D., London, British Museum).

The voyage of the Argo

The interpretation of the **Argonaut** myth, in line with the events of that far-off period, leads us to the conclusion that the bold Greek mariners undertook a whole series of exploits as they discovered the world through their voyages thereby increasing their geographical knowledge. The important discovery of the Euxine Pondus (all the areas around the Black Sea) and the spead of Hellenism to the countries there is what one derives from the narrations concerning the voyage and the route of the Argo.

After sacrificing to Apollo, the Argonauts embarked in the port of Pagasae. The omens for the voyage were good, and the ship set off. The first stop on their way was Lemnos, where they found the island women husbandless: all the men had been killed. The Argonauts formed unions with the women and helped them bear sons before sailing. After calling at Samothrace, they entered the Hellespont and reached Cyzicus. The king of the land, also called Cyzicus, and his people, the Dolioni, made the travellers very welcome. But when they tried to sail on, a head wind drove them back - and by a fatal misunderstanding, they failed to recognise the Doliani and the Doliani did not recognise them. There was a fierce battle in which Cyzicus and his subjects were massacred by the Argonauts. When they realised their mistake, it was too late, but each side, regretting what had happened, honoured the dead of the other.

The voyage of the Argo as described by Apollonius of Rhodes in his book on that expedition.

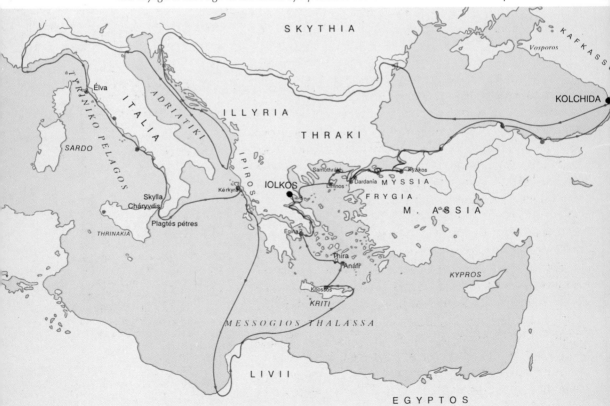

On the coast of Mysia, their next stop, the Nymphs abducted Hylas, beloved friend of Heracles. Heracles stayed on there with Polyphemus to search for his friend, and the rest of the company departed without them. Arriving in the country of the soothsayer Phineas, they freed him from the terrible Harpies, in return for which he revealed the future to them and told them how to deal with the Symplegades, the Clashing Rocks. The Symplegades were rocks which suddenly clashed together, crushing any ship which might happen to be passing between them at the time. Phineas told the Argonauts to release a dove and let it fly between the Symplegades first. If it managed to get through, then they would be able to follow it; if not, they were to hold back. Sure enough, the Argonauts released a dove and it flew through the gap, the Clashing Rocks managing only to knock a few feathers out of its tail. The Argo was similarly fortunate: it sailed between the rocks and escaped only with slight damage to its stern. In the end, after still more adventures, the Argo and her crew arrived in the country of king Aeëtes.

In this image the Argonauts are persuing the terrible Hapries, Aello and Ocypete, who are holding Phineas hostage. (Ivory relief figures from a Corinthian workshop, 570 B.C., Delphi, Archaeological Museum).

The **Harpies** were winged, rapacious spirits, half women and half bird with hooked talons. The Harpies seized children and souls. They played an important role in the myth of the seer Phineas whom they burdened with a curse: whatever he put on his table to eat was seized by the Harpies and whatever they were unable to seize they soiled with their excrement. Zetes and Calais, two of the Argonauts, liberated Phineas from the Harpies.

In Colchis

As soon as the company arrived in Colchis, Jason presented himself before king Aeëtes and told him of the orders he had received from Pelias. Aeëtes declared his willingness to part with the golden fleece - on condition that without any assistance Jason yoked two bulls given him by Hephaestus, which had bronze hooves and breathed fire, and then used them to plough a field and sow it with dragon's teeth which he would provide.

Medea, the daughter of Aeëtes and a sorceress, fell in love with Jason and, after making him promise to marry her, offered to help him. She gave him a magic ointment with which to smear his body and his shield before taking on the bulls. The ointment would make him impervious to fire and metal for a whole day. She also told him that the dragon's teeth would sprout at once and armed warriors would spring out of the ground to kill him. She advised him to stand at a distance and throw a stone among them, in which case they would kill each other in a quarrel over who had cast the stone.

Design depicting Jason endeavoring to tame the bull with the assistance of Medea.

With the help of Medea, Jason managed to accomplish the feat. But Aeëtes did not keep his word, and even tried to burn the Argo and kill the Argonauts. So Jason - once again with the help of Medea - put the dragon to sleep, stole the golden fleece, and set sail with all possible speed. As soon as Aeëtes discovered that Jason and Medea had fled - taking with them the golden fleece - he set off in pursuit of the Argo. In order to delay him, Medea killed her brother Apsyrtus (who had accompanied them) and, every so often, threw a part of his body into the sea.

The unfortunate Aeëtes lost time by stopping to collect the pieces of his beloved son, and soon the fugitives were out of danger.

Medea helping the hero to achieve his goal. In this depiction she diverts the dragon's attention, offering him drink to put him to sleep, at the same moment Jason manages to remove the golden fleece which is hanging on the branch of a tree. (Beginning of the 4th century B.C., Naples, Archaeological Museum).

The wanderings of the Argo

Aeëtes anchored off the shore of the Black Sea to bury his son, and the Argo sailed on. She passed the mouth of the Danube - which at that time was supposed to flow from the Adriatic to the Black Sea - and sailed up the rivers Eridanus (Po) and Rodanus to the lands of the Ligerians and the Celts before returning to the Mediterranean and arriving at the island of the Sirens. From afar the bewitching song of the Sirens reached their ears. But Orpheus of Thrace, the musician, struck his melodious lyre and sang in his sweet voice a song so beautiful that none of the Argonauts was tempted to succumb to the allures of the Sirens. Orpheus' nostalgic song was of their homes and their beloved ones who were waiting for them in their own lands, and it stirred in the companions the desire to sail home.

After many wanderings - which took them to the land of Circe, past Scylla and Charybdis, to the island of the Phaeacians and the coast of Libya - the Argonauts reached Crete, where they had to face the giant Talus, a creation of Hephaestus. Medea's spells and cunning helped them once again, and Talus, whom Minos set to guard his island against raiders, was vanquished.

A very beautiful depiction on a red-figured vase of the 5th century B.C. Jason is emerging from the mouth of a dragon half dead. Next to him is the goddess Athena and a bit further away can be seen the golden fleece, hanging on a tree. This representation refers to a variation of the myth which has not been preserved.

The Return to Iolkos

The company of friends sailed on across the Cretan Sea, entered the Aegean in foul weather and eventually came home to Iolkos, bearing with them the priceless golden fleece. Now the time had come for Jason to lay claim to the throne of King Pelias. But Pelias - who in the meantime had put all of Jason's relatives to death - refused to give up the throne to the rightful heir. So Jason was forced to resort to the magical powers and cunning of the witch Medea. She managed to gain entrance to the palace and set Pelias' daughters to kill him, tricking them into thinking they were taking part in a rite to rejuvenate their father. From this point on, we find a number of variations of the myth. In one, Jason and Medea ruled Iolkos and entrusted the son born to them to the Centaur Chiron; in another, they left the city and went to live in Corinth, after putting Acastus, Pelias' only son, on the throne.

Literary sources tell us that Heracles also took part in the Argonaut campaign. In this representation, he prepares himself for new labours along with his companion, Iolaus. (Black-figured tablet, 510-500 B.C., Athens, Archaeological Museum).

Jason with the golden fleece in his hands, returns to Iolkos where he is received by Peleus. (Apulian krater, 350-340 B.C., Paris, The Louvre).

The *Dioscouri* (sons of Zeus), Castor and Pollux, were born of Zeus' lovemaking with Leda. For her conquest Zeus turned himself into a swan. But the same night Leda made love to her husband Tyndareos, King of Sparta. Two sets of twins were born of this double mating; Pollux and Helen were thought to be the children of Zeus while Castor and Clytemnestra the children of Tyndareos. The Dioscouri took part in the Argonaut campaign. Castor was a warrior and Pollux a boxer.

103

PERSEUS

Perseus, son of Zeus and Danae, was a hero of Argos. His grandfather, Acrisius, once asked an oracle if he would ever have sons. The oracle replied that it would be the destiny of his daughter Danae to have a son who would kill him. In order to prevent this prophecy from coming true, Acrisius had Danae shut up in an underground cave with brass walls. But Zeus managed to squeeze through a crack in the cave - after transforming himself into a shower of golden rain - and formed a union with the lovely Danae. She gave birth to a son, whom she managed to bring up in secret for some months. When Acrisius found out about the baby, he refused to believe that Zeus had had anything to do with it; he killed Danae's wet-nurse, whom he suspected of complicity in the affair, and put his daughter and grandson in a wooden ark and set them adrift on the sea.

The Graiae were the only ones who were able to assist Perseus in his endeavor to get the head of Medusa. Thus, he very slyly seized their only eye and forced them to help him. In this representation, Perseus, who is found below, is attempting to seize the eye which the final Graia to the right is intending to give to her sister. (Cover of a pyxis, circa 425 B.C., Athens, Archaeological Museum).

Acrisius gives directions to the woodworker for the ark in which he intends to put Danae and the newborn Perseus. (Design for a red - figured hydria, circa 490 B.C.).

The waves washed them up on Seriphos, where the fisherman Dictes, brother of Polydectes, tyrant of the island, found it. Dictes took in Perseus and his mother, and it was in his house that the boy grew into a brave young men blessed with talents and gifts of all kinds. At one point King Polydectes fell in love with Danae, but he was never able to meet her because Perseus kept his mother well-guarded and the king felt unable to bring pressure to bear. Once, Polydectes invited Perseus to dinner with some other friends, and asked them what gifts they would give him if the need arose. All the young men answered that a horse was the most suitable gift for a king. Only Perseus answered that if it was absolutely necessary he would bring Polydectes the head of Medusa, the Gorgon. Polydectes pounced on this promise to demand that Perseus bring him the head of Medusa - otherwise, he said, he would seize Danae by force. And so Perseus set out to find the Gorgon and cut off her head.

Perseus decapitating Medusa. (Black-figured oinochoe, circa 540 B.C.).

Perseus' feat, and Perseus' revenge

The Gorgon, Medusa
There were three Gorgons: Stheno, Eurayle and Medusa. The first two were immortal and the third mortal. But the name Gorgon was primarily applied to Medusa. These monsters had snakes for hair, heavy tusks like wild boars, scales on their necks and golden wings so they were able to fly. They had such piercing eyes that whoever looked them straight in the face was turned to stone. These creatures were the cause of fear and loathing.

Athena and Hermes helped Perseus accomplish his feat. By a cunning trick, he managed to get the Nymphs to lend him winged sandals, a bag, and the helmet of Hades which would make him invisible. Hermes gave him a razor-sharp sickle. When Perseus came upon the Gorgons, they were asleep. Using the winged sandals, he swooped up high and cut off Medusa's head while looking at her reflection in the shiny shield which Athena had given him: if he had looked her straight in the eye, she would have turned him to stone. As soon as Medusa's head was off, Pegasus and the giant Chrysaor sprang from her neck. Perseus put the head in the bag and set off for home. Medusa's two sisters chased him, but in vain: wearing the helmet of Hades, Perseus was invisible.

On his way back, Perseus met Andromeda, a beautiful maiden whom he saved from the chains which bound her to a rock and the sea monster which was on the point of devouring her. Andromeda's parents agreed to a marriage between their daughter and her saviour, but Phineas, her uncle (who had been planning to wed her himself), began to plot against Perseus. As soon as Perseus realised what was going on, he produced the head of Medusa and turned Phineas and his fellow-conspirators to stone.

When Perseus got back to Seriphos, he took the same revenge on Polydectes, who, he was told, had been subjecting Danae to insufferable pressure.

Design depicting Perseus decapitating Medusa with the assistance of Athena.

Once Polydectes and his cronies had been turned to statues, Perseus put his adoptive father Dictes on the throne and, taking Andromeda with him, set out for Argos, his home, to meet his grandfather. But as soon as Acrisius heard of the approach of his grandson, he fled - yet he did not escape his fate. Later, he was present as a spectator at games in Larisa arranged by King Tentamides, at which Perseus was a competitor in the discus. When Perseus' turn came to throw, the discus slipped from his hand and hit Acrisius on the head, killing him. Perseus was grieved to learn who the dead man had been, and buried him with every honour.

Detail from the pediment of the temple of Artemis on Corfu which depicts a Gorgon wound with snakes. (Circa 590 B.C., Corfu, Archaeological Museum).

Design depicting Bellerophon mounted on Pegasus, attacking the Chimera with his spear.

The Chimera

Born of Typhon and Echidna it resembled both a goat and a lion. It is said to have had many goat's heads and one of a lion with a snake for a tail. Terrible in appearance, flames shot from its mouths and its nostrils. It plundered crops and did great damage. The Chimera was so dangerous that Iobates believed he had sent Bellerophon to certain death by asking him to exterminate it.

BELLEROPHON

ellerophon was actually the son of Poseidon, but among men his father was taken to be Glaucus, son of Sisyphus, of the royal house of Corinth. His mother was Eurynome, daughter of King Nisus of Megara. This hero acquired his name after killing a tyrant of Corinth called Bellerus (Bellerophon = the killer of Bellerus).

After the murder, he was forced to leave Corinth and seek out King Proetus of Tiryns, to expiate his crime. But when he was staying there Anteia, the wife of Proetus, fell in love with the young and handsome penitent - who denied her, out of respect for her husband's hospitality. To revenge this slight, Anteia went to Proetus and accused Bellerophon of having tried to seduce her, demanding that her husband put him to death.

Proetus decided to send Bellerophon - who, we should remember, was the owner of the winged horse Pegasus - to his father-in-law Iobates in Lycia, since he himself was prevented by the unwritten laws of hospitality from killing the youth. Iobates welcomed Bellerophon with feasting, and declared nine days of celebrations in his honour, during which time he sacrificed nine bulls as part of the rites in honour of his guest. On the tenth day he opened the letter from his son-in-law. It occurred to him, when he read Iobates' request that Bellerophon be put to death, that he could ask him instead to kill the Chimera, a terrible beast which had been reared by Amisodares, king of Caria. Bellerophon agreed to undertake the task. His greatest difficulty was with the fiery breath of the Chimera, which could throw its flames a considerable distance. But here he was helped by Pegasus, who soared up high with his rider and allowed Bellerophon to shoot the Chimera with his arrows from a safe distance.

After the Chimera had been dealt with, Iobates next commanded that Bellerophon be sent to fight the people called the Solymi, a fierce and belligerent tribe. Once they had been annihilated, the next order was to fight the Amazons. They, too, were defeated. Iobates was nearing despair, and his last attempt to kill Bellerophon consisted of the formation of a crack unit of troops whom he set to lie in ambush for the hero. But Bellerophon beat them, just as he had all the others. These feats convinced Iobates that Bellerophon must be of divine descent. He disclosed the instructions that Proetus had sent him, and out of respect and admiration for Bellerophon kept him by his side, married him to his daughter and, later, left him his kingdom.

The children of Bellerophon by Philonoe, daughter of Iobates, were Isandros, Hippolochus, and Laodamia, their only daughter. Hippolochus was the father of Glaucus, and Laodamia was the mother of Sarpedon, who commanded the Lycian army in the Trojan War. The two grandsons of Bellerophon distinguished themselves in the Trojan War, as Homer tells us in **The Iliad**, and their story is one of the pieces of evidence that point to a common origin for both the Achaean and Trojan sides.

Bellerophon met his end much later, we are told. His arrogance became such that he decided to fly up to the summit of Olympus on his winged steed, to see the house of Zeus and perhaps even take part in the councils of the gods. But Zeus was enraged by the hero's vanity, and Pegasus, the divine horse, threw his rider from the peak of the mountain. Then he returned to Olympus, where his true place was. From then on, he served Zeus by bringing him thunderbolts and helped Eo (the Dawn) when the time came for the day to break. In Corinth and Lycia, Bellerephon was treated as a hero white in **The Iliad** Homer mentions he had cordial relations with Oceanus, the king of Calydon.

Pegasus

Pegasus was the marvelous winged creature who, according to myth, sprang from the throat of Medusa when Perseus cut off her head, along with the hero Chrysaor, who with Bellerophon was a son of Poseidon, the only difference being that his ancestor Sisyphus was mortal. Bellerophon asked his father for a winged horse and his father gave it to him. But no bridle had yet been found to catch and hold this superb animal. Then the goddess Athena gave him a gold bridle with which he was able to tame the winged Pegasus. The hero then made a sacrifice to Poseidon.

Bellerophon on Pegasus. (Athens, Archaeological Museum).

DAEDALUS AND ICARUS

The Athenian craftsman Daedalus was a member of the royal family of Cecrops, first king of Athens. He was an artist of the greatest importance: he produced sculptures, works of architecture and some of the greatest inventions of his day. But for all his talents, the master craftsman once committed a crime against Talus, his nephew and apprentice. One day, Talus - who had already shown promise of developing into as great a craftsman as his father - was inspired to invent the saw by watching the way a snake used its jaws. Daedalus, blinded by envy, threw Talus off the Acropolis. When the crime came to light, the Areius Pagus - the supreme court of ancient Athens - sentenced Daedalus to exile.

And so Daedalus found himself in the service of King Minos of Crete, for whom, among other marvels he constructed the famous Labyrinth, a palace whose corridors were so complicated that it was impossible to retain one's bearings. It was in this maze that Minos enclosed the Minotaur.

While living in Crete, Daedalus had a son, Icarus, with a slave-woman in the palace, named Naucrate.

When Theseus came to Crete in order to kill the Minotaur, it was Daedalus who showed Ariadne how best to advise the hero on entering and leaving the Labyrinth. When Minos found out what he had done, he was so furious that he shut the artist and his son up in the Labyrinth themselves. There, in prison, Daedalus never ceased to think about ways in which he could escape from Crete. One day the thought of wings struck him. He stuck the feathers together with wax and fitted them to the shoulders of himself and Icarus, and the two set off on their incredible journey.

But young Icarus was deaf to his father's advice: Daedalus had told him not to fly too low in case his wings touched the wave-crests and got wet, or too high, so that the sun would not get them too hot. But Icarus, in his arrogance, flew higher and higher - until the wax in his wings melted in the heat of the sun and he plunged into the sea. That part of the ocean has ever since been called the Icarian Sea. Icarus' body was washed ashore on an island called Icaria since that time, and Heracles found and buried it.

The island of Icaria, Which took its name from Icarus, is a very beautiful island in the north Aegen. It was first settled by the Ionians at the end of the 9th century B.C.

The multi-faceted and inventive talents of Daedalus enabled him to devise and make the wings that would help him and Icarus fly far away from their prison and thus become the first humans to fly up to the sky.

The fall of Icarus, from a wall painting at Pompey.

ORPHEUS

Orpheus of Thrace was one of the protagonists in the Argonaut adventure. He is also the central figure in a highly symbolic myth with more religious features about it than any other of its time. The son of Oeagrus and (probably) the Muse Calliope, Orpheus was a charismatic musician, poet and singer. Apart from being a superb performer on the lyre, he was credited with inventing the cithara, the ancient guitar. The most familiar myth about Orpheus is that which tells of his descent into Hades in search of his beloved wife Eurydice. It goes as follows. Eurydice was a beautiful nymph of the woods. One day, she was running away from the attentions of Aristaeus, along the bank of a river, when she trod on a po sonous snake. It bit her, and she died. Orpheus, inconsolable, descended into Hades to find her and bring her back to life. His music charmed the entire Underworld, and all the souls in torment there forgot their punishments for a little while. Sisyphus, Tantalus, the Danaids and all the others rested from their eternal tortures to listen with delight to the music. Hades and Persephone agreed to let Eurydice go, but on one condition: that as Orpheus was ascending to the upper world once more, with Eurydice behind him, he must not turn round to look at her until they were safely out of the Underworld. But just before they emerged into the sunlight, Orpheus' anxiety to make sure that the shade of Eurydice really was behind him overcame him, and he turned round to make absolutely sure the gods of the underworld had not tricked him. Then everything was lost for ever; Eurydice joined the dead with no hope of return, and Hades turned a deaf ear to the pleas of the tragic figure of Orpheus.

After that time, there are many tales of Orpheus the nconsolable widower. He is said to have turned his back on world-

Design showing Orpheus playing his lyre.

ly things, of refusing to re-marry, of avoiding women and their love for three years. According to tradition, his only companions were Thracian boys, to whom he taught the 'Orphic life': abstinence from the consumption of meat, and initiation into music and the experiences which Orpheus himself had had in the underworld.

As for the death of Orpheus, the myths tell us that he become involved in a succession of relationships with men. This provoked the women whom he had spurned since the death of Eurydice to a frenzy of revenge: armed with stones and clubs, they came upon him one day defenceless, with only his lyre, attacked him and tore him to pieces. The Muses buried his remains and wept for him. Tradition has much to tell of this melodious singer, whose divine voice could charm even the elements of nature.

The end of Orpheus nears as a woman attacks him with her sword. (Red-figured amphora, 450-440 B.C., Paris, The Louvre).

PHAETHON

There are many stories about Phaethon, son of Helios the sun-god. Many versions have him as the son of Auge and Cephalus, but in the most common myth he is the offspring of Helios and the Oceanid Clymene, who brought him up without his father knowing of his very existence. When Phaethon reached adolescence, his mother revealed the truth to both father and son. Young Phaethon wanted proof of his paternity, however, and asked his father to let him drive the chariot of the sun. Helios refused, at first, but eventually gave in, bombarding the young man with instructions and advice.

To begin with, Phaethon took the route Helios used every day, but when he had gained height he took fright at the drop beneath him. The proximity to the signs of the Zodiac scared him, too, and he changed course. The chariot began to veer wildly about the sky, sometimes coming so low it was in danger of setting fire to the earth, and sometimes soaring so high it nearly scorched the stars. To put an end to this menace, Zeus let loose a thunderbolt and shot Phaethon down into the river Eridanus, where his sisters, the Heliads, buried him with all the honours due to the dead.

The famous operas Orfeo ed Euridice and Orfeo were works by the German composer Gluck, inspired by the Greek myth.

The great tragedian Euripides wrote a tragedy called Phaethon inspired by the myth. This is, unfortunately, one of the works that has not survived except perhaps in a few scattered fragments.

THE ROYAL HOUSE OF THE LABDACIDS

The royal house of the Labdacids, named after Labdacus, the grandson of Cadmus (who was the founder of Thebes) held a special place in the Theban Cycle. **Oedipus**, *the dominant figure in the family, along with its other members, have come to create classical characters by means of their adventures.*

OEDIPUS

The tragic hero Oedipus plays a central part in many stories which have come down to us, and above all in three of the most famous ancient tragedies. Oedipus was descended from Cadmus, the first king of Thebes; his great-grandfather was Polydorus, son of Cadmus, his granfather was Labdacus, and his father was Laius, all of them kings of Thebes.

Laius married Jocasta, daughter of Menoiceus and sister of Creon. Time passed, however, and Laius and Jocaste had had no sons. So the king went to the oracle, as was the custom then. The oracle told him that the couple would indeed have a son, but that he would bring great misfortune upon Thebes, killing the king, his father, and marrying his mother.

After this time, Laius kept well away from his wife. But Jocasta wanted a child more than anything else in the world, and so she got Laius drunk at a feast and spent the night with him. As soon as he discovered that the queen was with child, Laius began to think of ways of ridding himself of a baby which was a threat both to him and his country. As soon as the little boy was born, he pierced the infant's legs at the ankles, passed a chain through the holes and tied its legs together. Then he ordered a faithful shepherd to expose the baby in the forest on Mount Cithairon, where it would die of hunger and cold or might be devoured by some wild beast. But the shepherd took pity on the crying baby and, when some horse-traders in the service of king Polybus of Corinth came through the forest, he gave it to them without saying who it belonged to. The horse-traders took the baby to Polybus and his wife, who - childless themselves - were only too glad to look after it. Queen Merope gave the boy the name Oedipus, which means 'swollen-footed', because his legs had swelled up where Laius had pierced them to put on the chains.

In order for Cadmus to found Thebes, in agreement with the terms of the oracle, he had to face the dragon of the town. (Design on a Laconian disk, 550 B.C., Paris, The Louvre).

Cadmus, the hero of the Theban Cycle, and the son of Agenor and Telephassa was also the brother of Cilix of Phoenicia and Europa. After the abduction of Europa by Zeus, Agenor sent his sons to find her. Leaving Tyre, Cadmus wandered for quite some time until at last following the advice of the Delphic Oracle, he founded the town of Thebes the acropolis of which was called the Cadmeia. There are numerous accounts of his feats. He had many children from his marriage to Harmony: Autonoe, Ino (Leucothea), Agave, Semele (the mother of the god Dionysus), and Polydorus, the father of Labdacus.

Oedipus solving the riddle of the Sphinx. (Interior of a red-figured cylix, 470-460 B.C., Rome, Vatican Museum).

The Destiny of Oedipus

And so fate had it that Oedipus lived, and that he grew up to become a strong, clever young man who believed that Polybus and Merope were his parents. His real ancestry was kept a secret - until one day when, during a quarrel, someone who wanted to insult Oedipus told him that he was illegitimate and that the royal couple of Corinth were not his true parents. Unable to learn anything further from Polybus and Merope, Oedipus set out secretly to learn the truth from the Delphi oracle.

The oracle was its usual impenetrable self; but it did reveal to him that his terrible destiny would be to kill his father one day and marry his mother, and that both he and his descendants would be the source of great misfortune. Yet since nothing had been said about his ancestry, Oedipus continued to treat Polybus and Merope as his parents. Thus, so as to ensure that the oracle would not come true, he decided to stay away from Corinth. He set out on wanderings that took him to many places and saw him perform a multitude of feats.

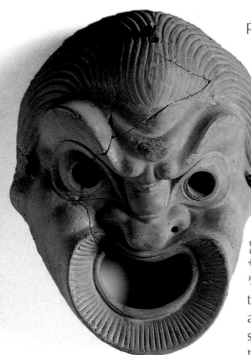

Mask from ancient drama.

Once, when he was travelling in Phocis, he came to a place where three roads met, and on the narrow road was a chariot guarded by armed men. It was none other than Laius, on his way to Delphi to find out what had happened to his son, since he was tormented by uncertainty as to whether the child had actually died. A quarrel arose when the king's men ordered the stranger to move aside to let the chariot past; Oedipus clashed with the guards and killed Laius and all his entourage - with the exception of one soldier, who managed to slip away.

Oedipus on the Throne of Thebes

At Thebes, Creon, Jocasta's brother, ruled with her after the death of Laius. But before they could begin searching for the murderer, the terror of the Sphinx engulfed the city. This monster sat on a rock at the edge of Thebes and asked passers-by a riddle - and since none of them could solve it, the Sphinx devoured them. Creon announced that anyone who could solve the riddle and rid Thebes of the terrible monster would become king and marry the queen.

Oedipus, still wandering, found himself in Thebes. He was told about the Sphinx, and decided to try his luck. The riddle was as follows: "What creature of earth is it which has four legs, three legs and two legs, and is weaker the more legs it has?" Oedipus solved the problem, replying that the creature is man, who crawls on all fours as a baby, walks on two legs when he is grown, and rests on a third leg - a walking-stick - when he becomes old.

After Oedipus had solved the riddle, the Sphinx flung itself from the rock and died. As the joyful news spread, the Thebans assembled and welcomed their hero, honouring the offer of the throne. Oedipus became king, and married Jocasta. Their union produced four children: Eteocles, Polynices, Antigone and Ismene. Oedipus' reign was a peaceful one - until an epidemic broke out in the country and people began to die like flies. There seemed no way of preventing this decimation, and Oedipus, in despair, sent Creon, his wife's brother, to ask the oracle what was causing the epidemic and what could be done to save Thebes from it. The answer came back that Thebes would be saved when Laius' murderer had been driven out.

Sophocles, the famous ancient tragadian, was inspired by the "Oedipal" myth to write several memorable tragedies: Oedipus Tyrannus, Oedipus at "Colonus" and "Antigone" while the tragedy "Phoenissae" was a product of the imagination of Euripides. Furthermore, global literature and art have not come up empty-handed in regard to such an interesting subject. Senea later wrote "Oedipus" and "Phoenissae" while the themes of the Oedipal myth were also taken up by Corneille, Voltaire, Gide, Cocteau, and Anouilh. Furthermore, Stravinsky, in collaboration with Cocteau wrote the opera-oratorio, "Oedipus" Tyrannus.

Statues of Sphinx.

And so Oedipus himself began to investigate the affair of Laius' murder. Although things looked promising at first, he was eventually forced to enlist the help of the sooth-sayer Tiresias - who revealed that Oedipus himself was the man the oracle had meant. There could be no doubting this revelation: the word of the blind seer was accepted throughout Greece. To begin with, Oedipus had his doubts, and wondered whether the accusation might be a plot on the part of Creon. Then he thought of fleeing to Corinth, but he was held back by the oracle which had said he was to kill his father and marry his mother. But before long news came from Corinth that Polybus had died, and that the people of the city wanted Oedipus to succeed him on the throne. Yet still Oedipus was afraid that the second half of the prophecy might come true - that is, that he might marry his mother. But the messenger who had brought the news told him not to worry about that, since Polybus was not his real father and the messenger himself had taken Oedipus, as a baby, to the palace at Corinth after receiving him from one of Laius' shepherds on Cithaeron.

The **Sphinx** was a legendary monster with the head of a woman, the legs and tail of a lion and the wings of a bird of prey. She was the daughter of Orthrus, the hound of Geryon, and Echidna and the sister of the other monsters (the Lion of Nemean, the Lernaean Hydra and the Chimera). Others say her father was Typhon. Hera sent this monster to Thebes to punish Laius because he had fallen in love with Chrysippas, the son of Pelops.

Then the shepherd who had hidden the baby was found, and his account explained the scars which could still be seen on Oedipus' legs, proving beyond doubt what had happened. Oedipus realised that he really had killed his father and married his mother. Jocasta, filled with horror at what had been done, retired to her own rooms and hanged herself; her son (and husband) followed her indoors, took off the gold brooches from her dress and stuck their pins into his eyes, blinding himself. He begged Creon to drive him out of Thebes, imploring him also to look after Oedipus' two daughters, Antigone and Ismene. Then Oedipus came as a suppliant to Colonus, in Attica, where the kind Theseus gave him shelter. Oedipus ended his days in Attica, bringing - as yet another oracle had foretold - great good to the city where he died.

Oedipus and the Sphinx. (Attican lecythus from Thebes, beginning of the 5th century B.C., Paris, The Louvre).

The Children of Oedipus

Oedipus' children Eteocles, Polynices, Antigone and Ismene were burdened by the curse of the incestuous relationship between their father and his mother Jocasta. All of them came to a bad end, and the boys had been cursed by their own father for their cruelty towards him during the last, unhappy moments of his life.

Initially, Eteocles and Polynices left their uncle Creon on the throne of Thebes. Later, however, they decided to take power into their own hands, ruling year in and year out. But the time came when Eteocles refused to relinquish power; the brothers quarrelled, and Polynices went into self-imposed exile. He took himself to Argos, where the king was called Adrastus, married the king's daughter and organised the campaign which was to become known as 'Seven Against Thebes'. It was given that name because seven chieftains led the army whose purpose was to defeat Thebes and put Polynices back on the throne. In the battle which ensued, the force besieging Thebes was beaten and both brothers were killed - at each other's hand.

This was the point at which Antigone, the dynamic and courageous sister of the dead sons of Oedipus, appeared on the scene. Creon had given orders that Eteocles was to be buried with all honour, while the corpse of Polynices, who had made war on his own city, was to be left to the vultures as punishment for his crime and as a lesson to others.

Antigone defied the king's orders; faithful only to the divine and moral law, which as she herself said is inalienable and immutable, she took upon herself the task of conducting Polynices' funeral rites and interring his corpse.

Although she was betrothed to Creon's son Aemon, Creon ordered that she be buried alive when his guards came upon her violating the royal order. Antigone hanged herself in the prison where she had been locked up, and Aemon, in his grief, killed himself over her body. As for little Ismene, it is said that she was killed by Tydeus, one of the Seven of the siege of Thebes, who found her making love to her sweetheart, Periclymenus the son of Poseidon, in a temple of Athena. Tydeus' steps were guided to the temple by Athena herself, who was furious that lovers should use her temple as a place of assignation. Her rage was further increased by one of the couple being the son of Poseidon, her great rival.

The funeral monument
on this pottery must refer to
Oedipus. Antigone is coming
to the tomb with offerings while
a young man (obviously Polynices
or Eteocles) is also approaching to
offer a band. (Luclian amphora, th
century B.C., Paris, The Louvre).

120

THE ROYAL HOUSE OF THE PELOPIDS

*Along with the royal house of the Labdacids there was the royal house of the **Pelopids**, which took its name from Pelops, the son of Tantalus. It was the leading force in the towns of the Peloponnese, which were then at their peak, places such as Argos, Mycenae and Corinth, to name a few.. The **Atreids,** whom we will speak of below, were the main Pelopids.*

The Family of the Atreids

Pelopas competing with his swift horse in a charmot race and as victor won the daughter of Oinomaos, Hippodamia, who became his wife. In this scene of supplication, Poseidon is emerging from the sea in all his majesty mounted on a sea-horse and fulfilling the request of his favourite Pelops who called for his help when he saw that only with divine assistance would he defeat Oenomaus in the chariot race. (Red-figured hydria, after 400 B.C., New York, Metropolitan Museum).

Pelops and Hippodameia were the parents of Atreus, Thyestes, Pleisthenes, Pittheus (grandfather of Theseus) and Niceppe (mother of Eurystheus, uncle of Heracles). After the death of Eurystheus, who had succeeded to the throne of his father Sthenelus, the Pelopids became much more powerful and ruled in Mycenae, Tiryns, Argos and the Argolid.

According to one version of the story, Pelops passed on the sceptre of power to Atreus, his first-born. When Atreus died before succeeding and with sons who were not of age, Pelops gave the sceptre to his brother, Thyestes. As a good guardian should, Thyestes passed it on in his turn to Agamemnon, his late brother's eldest son, and not to his own son. However, there is also an account in which the Pelopids were an accursed family, because of the events which we shall now relate.

Before Atreus and Thyestes came to rule in the Argolid, they were exiled to Triphylia under the curse of Pelops because they had killed his illegitimate son Chrysippus, fearing that their aged father, who doted on him, might leave him the throne. As soon as the two brothers arrived in Triphylia, Thyestes suggested that they propose to the local nobility that they should recognise as their king the possessor of a golden fleece which was a gift from Hermes. Atreus had no objection to this, since it was to him that Hermes had given the fleece. But Thyestes knew what he was doing: he had persuaded Atreus' wife Aerope, with whom he was having an affair, to give him the fleece so that he would become king. Zeus, however, did not wish to see such an injustice take place, and so he advised Atreus to make a bet with Thyestes: that on the following morning the sun would rise in the west. Thyestes, of course, accepted, and the sun's course was changed by the will of Zeus so that Atreus would win the bet. He ascended the throne, and Thyestes left Triphylia. But in the end Atreus found out about the secret affair between his brother and his wife, and he thought up a terrible way of taking his revenge.

He invited Thyestes to come back to Triphylia, supposedly so the two brothers could be reconciled, and at dinner he served him the roast flesh of his children, whom he had slaughtered and dismembered. When the banquet was over, he told Thyestes what he had been eating. In disgust a this awful and revolting vengeance, Thyestes overturned the table and laid a heavy curse on the house of the Atreids. The phrase 'a Thyestian banquet' passed into the language as a concise way of describing a disproportionately frightful act of revenge.

Thyestes wished to pay his brother back for what he had done. He was told by an oracle to have a child by his own daughter, and the child would take revenge on the Atreids. And so he deliberately (or perhaps involuntarily, while drunk after a feast) formed a union with his daughter Pelopia - and the fruit of their incestuous loins was Aegisthus, who when he was grown killed Atreus and put his father Thyestes on the throne of Mycenae.

The Sons of Atreus

After their father's death, Atreus' sons Agamemnon and Menelaus took refuge in Sikyon. At some later date, Tyndareus, father of Castor and Pollux, Clytemnestra and Helen, helped Agamemnon to regain the throne which was his by right. Thyestes and his son Aegisthus were exiled, and Agamemnon took Clytemnestra as his wife - after she had first killed Tantalus, her first husband, who was also a son of Thyestes. Agamemnon and Clytemnestra had three daughters - Iphigenia, Electra and Chrysothemis - and one son, Orestes. Menelaus married the beautiful Helen and ruled in Sparta.

The children of Atreaus Agamemnon was the most illustrious of the Atreids. Aschylus was inspired by his personality in the tragedy "Agamemnon", which is the first part of the trilogy The "Orestia" (Agamemnon - Choephori - "Eumenides"). A tragedy called Agamemnon was also written by the Italian lyric poet Alfierri.

Agamemnon an libation vase.

THE TROJAN WAR

ITS CAUSES

THE ACHAEAN CAMPAIGN AGAINST TROY

The Trojan campaign was the great war that threw that far-off period into confusion. This terrible conflict lasted for ten years and cost the life of many heroes. The Achaeans and the Aeolians, Greeks from continental Greece, laid seige to and defeated the Trojans, Greeks from Asia Minor. Myth relates that the Trojan war was fought for the love of the beautiful Helen. Nevertheless, the war itself was not a myth as was shown by the excavations of archaeologists which brought to light all the things that Homer speaks of in **The Iliad**. Today the whole world knows that the Achaeans went to the coast opposite them with the full weight of their military forces to defeat fertile and civilized Troy. They were strong and brave so shouldn't they be able to make this wealth theirs, to carry its lovely women off to their own homes and take whatever beautiful thing Ilium had to offer? Moreover, there were no difficulties in making contact with and communicating as the Trojans belonged to the same race and indeed were relatives.

Paris and Helen in a drawing by the French painter Nadar.

The Achaeans had an army of 100,000 - 135,000 and a fleet of 1,186 ships. All the leaders of the Achaeans and the Aeolians took part in the campaign. The Trojans had an amazingly well fortified town and the assistance of their own allies. These were neighboring peoples who were both of foreign and Greek races: Lyceans, Myseans, Cicones, Paplagonians, Phrygians, Maeonians, Carians, Pelasgians, Thracians, Assyrians and Ethiopians and perhaps even some Egyptians.

Famous Homeric heroes made their mark in this war: Achilles, the dominant figure of **the Iliad**, Agamemnon, Odysseus, Hector, Paris and many others.

Ancient historians believed the main cause of the Trojan War was the quest for new lands, because after the descent of the Dorians in 1100 B.C., Greece was faced with threats to its survival.

But the myth surrounding this war takes us back to events which are worth relating. Everything began at a wedding feast, the wedding of Peleus and Thetis.

Relief amphora from Tinos with a variety of representations from the Trojan War. Dated to around 670 B.C. and found on Mykonos. (Archaeological Museum, Mykonos).

The Marriage of Peleus and Thetis

eleus was the king of Phthia, where the Myrmidons lived. An old myth relates that the Myrmidons ruled by Peleus and his father Aeacus had once been ants, which were transformed into human beings to people the kingdom.

Peleus married Thetis, goddess of the sea. All the gods came to the wedding, to present their gifts and take part in the banquet. Only one divinity had been left out: Eris, goddess of controversy and discord. To avenge this slight, Eris chose her moment and tossed a golden apple in front of three of the goddesses: Hera, Athena and Aphrodite. The apple - said to have come from the garden of the Hesperides - bore an inscription: "To the most beautiful". Naturally enough, a quarrel broke out among the three goddesses, each of whom claimed the apple. As fate would have it, the dispute over the apple led to the fall of Troy and the dissolution of Mycenae, both of them flourishing cities. Far away in the Troad, beyond the Hellespont, Paris, the young prince who was the son of king Priam, was tending his flocks.

This scene shows a representation of the wedding procession of Peleus and Thetis from the François vase. (Circa 570 B.C., Florence Museum).

Zeus ordered Hermes to give Paris the difficult job of judging which of the three goddesses ought to receive the golden apple, after he had weighed all the graces of each in the balance. The goddesses offered the young prince the gifts that were in their power: Hera, rule over Asia and Europe, Athena, heroism and victory - and Aphrodite, love, in the person of the lovely Helen.

Paris had never seen Helen. But her reputation was so great, and his desire for love so strong, that he unhesitatingly awarded the apple to the beautiful Aphrodite. The other two goddesses were angry, and after that time supported the Achaeans against the Trojans in the war which was to ensue. Aphrodite gave Paris her advice as to how best to conquer Helen.

The union of Peleus and Thetis produced Achilles, who was destined to be the greatest of the heroes of the Trojan War. Thetis wished to make her son immortal, and so she dipped him in the waters of the sacred river Styx, holding him by the heel. As a result, he was vulnerable at that point, and the phrase 'Achilles' heel' is still used today to describe someone's weak point. Peleus took his son to Chiron, the Centaur, who taught him how to hunt wild animals, the arts of war, music, painting and all the other things there were to be learned at that time.

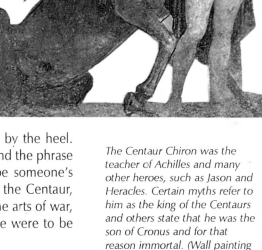

The Centaur Chiron was the teacher of Achilles and many other heroes, such as Jason and Heracles. Certain myths refer to him as the king of the Centaurs and others state that he was the son of Cronus and for that reason immortal. (Wall painting from the Herculaneum).

Peleus abducts Thetis while she is bathing in a spring. (Etruscan krater, circa 340 B.C., Rome).

Peleus entrusts the education of the small Achilles to the Centaur Chiron.
(Black-figured lecythus circa 500 B.C. Athens, Archaeological Museum).

The Trojans

he fortress of Troy stood on Mt. Ida, on the far side of the Hellespont. It had been built for Laomedon by Poseidon and Apollo. At the time when the events we are relating occurred, Troy was ruled by Priam, son of Laomedon, whose wife was called Hecuba. Priam had originally been named Podarces ('fine-legged'), and he was the brother of Hesione, who had followed Telamon to Salamis, married him, and borne him Teucrus and Ajax, both of whom were to fight in the Trojan War. As can be seen, the Achaeans and the Trojans were not only members of the same race, sharing a language, religion and customs, but often had family bonds, as well. Priam, ruler of the fortified city of Troy, had more children than any other ruler mentioned in the myths: fifty sons, and countless daughters. His first-born son was Hector, followed by Paris, Deiphobus, Hellen, Polydorus and Troilus; the best-known of his daughters were Creousa, Laodice, Polyxene, and Cassandra, who was gifted with the power of divination.

Tros the hero who gave his name to the people of Troy, was the son of Erichthonius, the grandson of Dardanus, while Astyoche was his mother. He married Callirrhoe, daughter of Scamandrus and had a daughter called Cleopatra (Cleopatra is a Greek name) and three sons: Ilos who founded the acropolis of Ilium, Assaracus and Ganymede, who was loved by Zeus.

Priam originally married Arisbe with whom he had Aesacus. Then he left her and married Hecuba. Hecuba was exceptionally fertile. Though ancient writers are not in agreement over the number of children she had, the family she had with Priam was a very large one.

Priam and Hecuba seated on their throne receive the sorrowful news of the murder of their son Troilus with heart-stricken gestures. (Shard from a Clauzomenian hydria, circa 540 B.C., Athens, Archaeological Museum).

Paris and Helen

Helen and Paris in a drawing by the Frenchman Nadar.

As we have already seen, Agamemnon, king of Mycenae, married Clytemnestra, and Menelaus took her sister Helen. Menelaus was king in Sparta, and that was where he welcomed Paris and his entourage when they arrived bearing precious gifts. As soon as Paris set eyes on Helen, he was dazzled by her beauty. Menelaus honoured the young prince from abroad in accordance with the customs of hospitality, but on the tenth day after Paris' arrival he was forced to leave for Crete. Paris seized the opportunity to make his advances to Helen, who was unable to resist the power wielded by Aphrodite. She accepted the treasures which Paris offered her, and agreed to run away with him. The couple escaped by night and returned to Troy, where their wedding was celebrated. But Iris, messenger to the gods, brought the news to Menelaus in Crete.

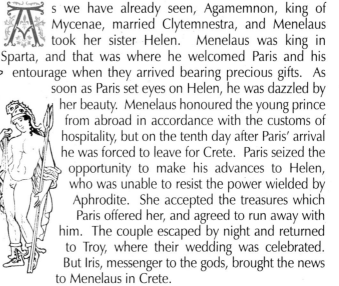

The Achaean Campaign Against Troy

As soon as Menelaus heard about Helen's flight he sailed away from Crete and went straight to his brother Agamemnon in Mycenae. The two kings - with Nestor, the wise ruler of Pylus - decided to raise all the kings and heroes of Greece in a campaign: it was a matter of honour. The ravisher of Helen must be punished, since otherwise, if such a breach of the rules of hospitality were condoned, no one could be entirely easy in his mind about his wife. Thus the insult which Paris offered Menelaus had to be taken as a personal affront. But here, too, the oracles and the prophecies of the soothsayers had their part to play, and those who knew what their fate was to be were reluctant to join the campaign. Odysseus, son of Laertes and king of Ithaca, was one of these men: he knew from the start that it would be twenty years before he returned home, and so when Agamemnon and Menelaus brought him the summons he pretended to have gone mad. He had recently married and had a baby son, Telemachus. When the two kings arrived, they found him dressed in outlandish clothing and behaving strangely, ploughing a field. But the cunning Palamedes proved he was only play-acting by laying the baby Telemachus on the ground in front of the plough: naturally enough, Odysseus could not carry the pretence of madness so far as to kill his own son.

Helen, the most beautiful woman in the world of that time, was desired by all the princes of Greece. Tyndareaus, her father, vacillated a great deal. Then following the advice of Odysseus, he decided to bind all the perspective suitors to an oath that they would accept the choice of Helen herself and that they would hasten to her assistance if the honour of her spouse was threatened. The Atreids invoked this oath when asking for the participation of so many heroes in the Trojan campaign. Using the theme of the Beautiful Helen, Euripides write his tragedy "Helena" in 412 B.C. The Italian neoclassical sculptor, Antonio Canova also made a statue called "Helen of Troy".

Achilles prepares for his great campaign against Troy: he is putting on his greaves and Thetis is holding his sword and his shield. (Black-figured tablet, circa 560 B.C., Athens Archaeological Museum).

Hephaestus was the one who made the weapons of Achilles, which he delivered to Thetis.

The mother of Achilles was equally unwilling to let her son go off to war. She sent him to Skyros, to the palace of king Lycomedes, where he lived for a while in female dress, with his girl cousins. It was a trick played by Odysseus that found him out: Odysseus took gifts of female clothing and jewellery to the palace, for the king's daughters, and hid a javelin and a shield among them. As Odysseus was showing these luxuries to the girls, he had the herald sound the call to battle. Achilles could not be restrained; he had already been handling the weapons, and now he seized them and made ready to attack. Once his disguise had been seen through, he went to Aulis with the rest of the expeditionary force. It took ten whole years to gather the flower of Greek manhood and military art at the harbour of Aulis. The heroes who joined the army included the wise Nestor, king of Pylos, Diomedes the hero of Aetolia, Ajax, the Telamonian, Ajax the Lorcian, Idas, King of Crete and Idomeneus.

131

The Sacrifice of Iphigenia - The Departure for Troy

Iphigeneia lived at Taurus as a priestess in the temple of the goddess Artemis until her brother came there with his friend Pylades. Orestes had a command from the Delphic Oracle to bring the statue of the goddess, which was in the land of Taurus, to Greece. He was soon in danger of being a victim of human sacrifice at the hands of his own sister but then they recognized each other and he returned to Greece with her and the statue. The myth of Iphigeneia was the subject of tragedies by Aeschylus, Euripides, Racine, Goethe and even the dance dramas "Iphigenie en Aulide" and "Iphigenie en Tauride" by Gluck.

At last the fleet was ready for departure in the harbour of Aulis. But the winds were not favourable: there was dead calm, and the ships were motionless. The seer Calchas was asked to divine the cause of the lack of wind, and he replied that the goddess Artemis was angry with Agamemnon for having killed a sacred deer in a grove where she was honoured. She was determined not to allow a following wind to blow unless Agamemnon sacrificed the beautiful Iphigenia, his elder daughter, to her. To begin with, Agamemnon refused even to countenance the idea. But the troops revolted, and so a plan prepared by Odysseus was put into motion. A message was sent to the palace at Mycenae, summoning Iphigenia to Aulis, with her mother, supposedly so that she could be married to Achilles. Clytemnestra, overjoyed at her daughter's sudden good fortune, hastened to Aulis. But what she found there was an altar, and the seer ready with his knife to make the sacrifice. Everything was got ready in an atmosphere of the greatest tension. But just as Calchas raised the knife, Artemis - whose unsleeping eye had been on the proceedings - bore Iphigenia off to Tauris (now the Crimea), where she became a priestess in the goddess's temple. A doe,

Representation of the sacrifice of Iphigeneia. Iphigeneia on the right approaches the altar while the hind that in the end will take her place has already begun to appear. (Apulian krater, 370 B.C., London, British Museum).

Depiction showing Menelaus attacking Paris (Circa 490 B.C., Paris, The Louvre).

symbolising the favour of the goddess, was sacrificed instead, to the delight of the troops. The wind immediately filled the sails of the ships, and the Greek fleet sailed out of Aulis on its way to Troy to expunge the disgrace which had been caused by Helen.

The Trojan War - The Iliad

The Achaeans, loyal to their religion and traditions, sacrificed before commencing hostilities in the Trojan War so as to allow the gods to indicate their will for the future and the outcome of the war. As the sacrifice was taking place, a snake appeared with a back as red as blood. The snake slithered off the altar and up a nearby plane tree. On the highest branch was a sparrow, with its young. The snake devoured all eight of the sparrow chicks, and then their mother. Once it had swallowed all nine birds, Zeus turned it to stone. The soothsayer Calchas had his interpretation of this unnatural event: the siege of Troy would last for nine years, and in the tenth the city would fall.

Troy, otherwise known as Ilium, was a place of murderous battles, protected by Apollo with his silver bow. The first casualty of the war was Protesilaus, on the Achaean side, to whom a monument was erected and who was buried with honours. The goddesses Athena and Hera helped the Achaean forces. Homer's epic The Iliad gives a detailed account of all the events in the Trojan War, many of which had as their protagonist Achilles, a hero renowned throughout the known world.

Protosilaus, the first victim of the Trojan War, was from Thessaly and had been one of the perspective suitors of Helen. He took part in the war with a fleet of forty ships. As he jumped from his ship at Troy he was shot down by Hector.

Achilles and the Quarrel with Agamemnon

The heroic figure of Achilles. (Detail from a red-figured amphora, 450 B.C., Rome, The Vatican).

Agamemnon,
the mightiest king of his time, took command of all the Achaean forces. His marriage to Clytemnestra sealed his doom. Clytemnestra was formerly the wife of Tantalus whom Agamemnon killed along with their newborn son. It was fated that a host of murders would follow in the family of the Atreids. As a warrior Agamemnon was brave and able and had many military gifts.

It was Achilles' fate to die in Troy, which was why his mother, Thetis, had initially been so unwilling for him to take part in the war. But Agamemnon, the commander-in-chief, moved heaven and earth to have Achilles and his fearful Myrmidons by his side.

During the nine years the Trojan War lasted, Achilles captured and looted quite a number of the cities around Troy and enslaved many beautiful women, whom he presented to Agamemnon. He kept only one slave for himself, Diomede; but she came second in Achilles' affections to Breseis, daughter of Breseus, whom he wished to marry when he returned to Phthia. Breseis, too, was a prisoner: she had been captured during a raid on the strong city of Thebes, together with another girl called Chryseida.

Chryseida was the daughter of Chryses, a priest of Apollo, and she rivalled Breseis in beauty and in the nobility of her descent. She had been promised to Agamemnon.

When news came to the priest Chrysis, in the island sanctuary of Apollo where he lived, of his daughter's capture, he dressed in his sacred vestments, took rich gifts as ransom, and set off for the Greek camp to buy back his daughter.

But Agamemnon was reluctant to part with Chryseida, and so he drove Chryses away with harsh words - thus incurring the wrath of Apollo.

The arrows from the god's silver bow rained mercilessly down on the Achaean camp, spreading the plague, first among the animals and then among the men. This was the beginning of the quarrel between Achilles and Agamemnon: Achilles said that it was Agamemnon's duty to send Chryseida back to her father, so as to put an end to the plague. In the end, most reluctantly, Agamemnon let Chryseida go - but then he snatched Breseis from Achilles, in the belief that one item of booty ought to be replaced by another.

Achilles, angered by this injustice, spoke intemperately to his commander-in-chief and then withdrew to his tent, where he sat refusing to take any part in the fighting. The Trojans were delighted to see the Greeks so divided amongst themselves, and with improved morale they decimated the Achaean ranks in battle. Now that Achilles and his Myrmidons were absent, the field of battle belonged to the Trojans.

Achilles' Revenge

In order to plead her son's cause, Thetis climbed Olympus to the throne of Zeus. She threw herself down before him, embracing his legs with her left arm and stroking his beard with the other, a customary way of expressing respect, subjugation and love. Thetis begged Zeus to give her son satisfaction - after all, his life was destined to be a very short one. She implored Zeus to let the Achaeans and Agamemnon see and appreciate Achilles' worth, and also to help Achilles overcome the insult which had been done to him. But no help came to the besiegers, and Apollo with his silver bow and the arrows of Hector and the other Trojans continued to spread death among the Achaeans.

In vain Patroclus, Achilles' closest friend, begged him to do something to stop the Trojans, who seemed likely to reach the Greek ships and burn them. But Achilles was adamant. He sat in his tent all day, refusing even to consider the possibility of joining the battle. And so it came about that his beloved friend Patroclus took the initiative of leading the Myrmidons into battle himself, wearing Achilles' armour so as to mislead the Trojans. Achilles' armour was unique: it had been made by Hephaestus himself, on the request of Thetis. When Patroclus went out to battle in Achilles' armour and with his weapons and chariot, the Trojans began in fear to retreat towards the walls of their city, believing that the king of the Myrmidons was on the battlefield once more.

Achilles had one son named Neoptolemus (Neoptolemus=young warrior) by Deidamia, daughter of the king of Skyros, Lycomedes. After the death of Achilles, Neoptolemus came to Troy and carried on the exploits of his father. He invented a Pyrrhic war dance, and was one of those to hide in the Trojan horse. After the fall of Troy, Neoptolemus took as his plunder Andromache, the widow of Hector and married Hermione, the daughter of Menelaos.

Modern wall painting from the Achilleio on Corfu in which Achilles is shown on his chariot dragging the dead Hector behind him.

Achilles and Ajax

Two heroes with much in common in terms of ethos, valour and intellectual cultivation. The great Heracles once passed through the kingdom of Telemon and asked Zeus to make the newborn Ajax invulnerable when he covered him with his lion skin. Ajax was indeed invulnerable except for his shoulder, sides and armpit, that is the parts which corresponded to where the quiver was on Heracles' body.

Achilles led fifty ships to Troy with his Myrmidons. Basides Patroclus he was also accompanied by the educator and advisor Phoenix who was at his side every moment. Thetis had warned her son about his brief life but also told him the glory that lay in store for him. Achilles himself never wavered in his decision to take part in the war.

*In the framework of their military undertaking, Achilles and Ajax play with dice in a version of the present-day backgammon.
(Black-figured amphora, 530 B.C., Rome, The Vatican).*

The beautiful Breseis, with her embroidered Ionian costume, and a flower in her hand, was the reason for the quarrel between Achilles and Agamemnon.

Patroclus succeeded in cutting off the Trojan advance before it reached the Greek camp and in striking some heavy blows against them. But as the Trojans fell back, Apollo told Hector that the man in the armour was not really Achilles - and Hector killed Patroclus. A fresh battle followed over the body of Patroclus, for his weapons and armour, which, by convention, were taken by the warrior who had killed him.

Menelaus distinguished himself in this fierce fighting. In the meantime, Antilochus son of Nestor had brought Achilles the news of the death of his friend. Achilles, in a frenzy of sorrow and rage, rushed out on to the battlefield unarmed. He let out a cry which so terrified the Trojans that they ran away and left the dead body of Patroclus unharmed.

In his grief over the death of his friend, Achilles forgot his personal differences with Agamemnon and thought of nothing but revenge. The day after Patroclus' death, he asked Agamemnon to overlook their quarrel, and announced that he was ready to fight by the side of the commander-in-chief

Athena stands between the two warriors, Achilles and Hector. (Paris, The Louvre).

To honour
the dead Patroclus,
Achilles organized a
chariot race in the name
of his friend. (Fragment from
a black-figured goblet,
570 B.C., Athens,
Archaeological Museum).

once more. Agamemnon apologised for his own behaviour, and returned Breseis to him, swearing a great oath that he had never laid a finger on her.

And so Achilles went into battle once more, scorning all the prophecies which had been made as to his imminent death. As soon as they saw him, the Trojans turned and fled. Only Aeneas stood his ground and fought in single combat with Achilles for a while, but Poseidon came between them and tricked them into separating. Achilles drew closer and closer to Troy. The Trojans mourned countless numbers of dead as the Achaean hero fought his way nearer to Hector, to revenge himself. After many battles and duels, he came upon Hector at the Scaean Gates. As the two warriors chased one another and prepared for battle, Zeus threw the fates of Achilles and Hector into the balance - and it was the destiny of Hector that dipped towards the underworld. And so it came about that in the duel Hector was killed. But Achilles' lust for revenge was still not quenched: he tied the corpse behind his chariot and dragged it round the city walls before returning to camp for Patroclus' funeral. Yet when Priam came as a supplicant to his tent, to beg the body of his son for burial, Achilles greeted the aged king and father of his enemy politely and

The personality of **Hector** is one of the highlights of The Iliad. He was the first among Trojans, endowed with unusual virtues. Homer was to make his patriotic statement immortal down through the centuries. When the oracular signs, the omens, did not foresee a good outcome for the battle, Hector said, "The best omen is for one to defend his homeland" (The Iliad, XII, 243).

Achilles takes care of his wounded friend Patroclus with great skill.

139

It is worth noting the presence in the Trojan War of two heroes named Ajax: **Ajax the Lorcian** and **Ajax the Telamonian**. **Ajax the Lorcian** was the head of the Lorcian forces which numbered forty ships. He was small in size (Lesser Ajax) when compared to the Greater Ajax, fought in all the famous battles in The Iliad but is considered to have had a bad character given to impiety and sacrilige. During the fall of Troy he violated the sanctuary of Athena going after Cassandra, the daughter of Priam. The gods punished him with death on his way back.

Ajax the Telamonian, the son of Telemon, the "Greater Ajax", was also a nephew of Priam (the mother of this hero was the sister of Priam). He was the king of Salamis and the head of twelve ships. He was composed, handsome, judicious and robust and the strongest man after Achilles. He is described as pious, a man of few words and of flawless character. Achilles got the better of him in terms of sensibility, the love of music and gentility because Ajax was a rough and ready warrior. In the competitions organized by Achilles he and Odysseus fought to a draw. Fate decreed that he was to die by his own hand, after he was seized by an attack of madness. According to another account, he was murdered. The great tragedians, Sophocles and Aaechylus narrate the events of his turbulent life in the tragedies they wrote about him, both called Ajax.

Priam comes to impore Achilles to give him the body of his son Hector which has been left on the ground.

respectfully. Forgetting all his enmity, he turned over the body of Hector for burial, issuing orders that it was to be treated in a manner fitting a brave warrior.

Priam, crushed by sorrow, took the body of his first-born son back to Troy, where Hector's wife Andromache and his mother Hecuba were waiting to inter it.

The Death of Achilles

The war before Troy continued. The terrible Achilles struck fear into the Trojans. In one incident, he fought a duel with Penthesilea, the famous queen of the Amazons, whom he wounded mortally. He was overcome with sadness at the sight of death drawing its veil across her beautiful face. There was also a duel with Memnon, son of Io - and a passing moment of love with Polyxene, daughter of Priam.

The courage and heroism of Achilles were unparalleled throughout the war. But, in the end, his death was fated to come. Achilles, at the head of his troops, had driven the Trojans back until they were at the walls of the city. Then Paris used the information which Apollo had given him and aimed his fatal arrow at the hero's only weak point: his heel. Achilles fell, and a murderous battle ensued over his body. In the end, Odysseus and Ajax managed to carry it back to the camp; at one point, Glaucus the grandson of Bellerophon attempted to drag the body off with a belt, but Ajax killed him. Thetis and the Nereids undertook the funeral ceremonies. The mourning for Achilles lasted seventeen days. His body was anointed with aromatic oils and scents, and Athena sprinkled it with ambrosia to stop it decomposing. (In another version, the body was embalmed.) On the eighteenth day, a fire was built and the mortal remains of the hero cremated. A magnificent tomb was built, and Achilles' ashes were placed in it, inside a gold amphora which also contained the ashes of his dearest friend, Patroclus.

Centuries afterwards, another hero - Alexander the Great, who had modelled himself on Achilles - sacrificed at the tomb, after making his devotions and crowning it with a wreath.

Paris did not enjoy the fruits of his feat for long. Death overtook him at the hands of Philoctetes, who thus avenged the death of Achilles and the insult which the rape of Helen had meant for the Greeks.

When **Alexander the Great** set off with his Greeks on his campaign into Asia he did not neglect paying homage to his idol. As a child with a wooden sword, Alexander had always wanted to play Achilles in his games. A field marshall by then, he kneeled at his grave and declared his secret desire to be like him. "How I envy you, son of Paleus, praised by the likes of Homer!"

The wounded Achilles tries to pull the fatal arrow out of his heel. (Modern statue from the royal gardens on Corfu).

Diomedes from Aetolia, who stood out among the Achaeans, met the highly gifted Galucus from the Trojan side. "Who are you" Diomedes asked. "I don't know you but I will defeat you". "I am Glaucus and my grandfather was the renowned Bellerophon, a rare and mighty man!" "If that is the case, then you are a friend". Diomedes replied. "Your grandfather came to the palace of my uncle Oeneus, was received as guest and then they became friends and exchanged gifts". The two antagonists shook hands, exchanged their weapons as gifts and a while later took up their old positions in the battle.

Detail from a relief amphora of the Trojan horse (Circa 670 B.C., Archaeological Museum of Mykonos).

143

The Fall of Troy - the Trojan Horse

After the death of Achilles, the besiegers of Troy were forced to ponder what they could do to bring the war to a favourable conclusion. Ten years had passed, and they were beginning to despair; their courage was not what it had been. It occurred to the wily Odysseus, king of Ithaca, that the city might best be captured by a trick. So he thought up a plan, gained the consent of the other leaders, and put it into effect. A huge wooden horse was built, with a hollow stomach. When it was finished, Odysseus and eight other warriors entered the stomach of the horse through a hidden trapdoor; the horse was left outside the Greek camp in a place where it could be seen from the Trojan walls, while the remainder of the Greek forces struck camp, burned their tents and sailed off. They did not go far, however; just to the islet of Tenedus, behind which they hid from view. The Trojans, watching the Greeks retreat, were unable to believe their eyes at first. Then they spied the wooden horse, which they approached with suspicion. It bore an inscription saying that the horse was dedicated by the Greeks to Athena. In vain Cassandra, daughter of Priam, prophesied that the horse would bring evil on the Trojans. No one was prepared to listen to her. Laocoon, priest of Apollo, hurled his javelin at the horse; it stuck in the stomach with a hollow, booming sound. He, too, tried in vain to persuade the Trojans not to trust the Achaeans. As he was speaking, the goddess Athena sent two huge serpents out of the sea, which suffocated Laocoon and his sons. The Trojans took this as a sign that the goddess would punish them if they failed to take the gift. So they towed it into the city. As soon as Troy was asleep, Odysseus and the others crept out of the wooden horse and opened the city gates. At the same time, the fleet sailed back and the Greeks launched an attack with all the force at their disposal. They rushed in through the open gates and, by the time the Trojans had realised what was happening, it was too late. In the midst of the general massacre and destruction, Odysseus slew Priam at the altar of Zeus. The city was burned and looted - and as the flames rose, Menelaus ransacked the royal apartments of Troy in search of his wife, who had been the cause of the entire war. When Paris was killed, Helen had married Demophobus, his brother, whom Menelaus slew that same night. Sword in hand, he rushed into Helen's rooms. She, expecting only

Troas, the hero who gave his name to the people of Troy, was the son of Erichthonios, grandson of Dardanos, and Astyoche was his mother. He married Callirrohe, the daughter called Cleopatra (Cleopatra is a Greek name) and three sons, Ilos who founded the acropolis of Illium, Assaracus and Ganymete, who Zeus fell in love with.

Aeneas, the son of Anchises and Aphrodite, was a hero of Troy, the bravest after Hector and he took part in all the important battles. The piety of Aeneas is fabled. When the Achaeans captured Troy they allowed Aeneas because of his bravery to choose from among his possessions one thing to take with him as he left. The victors were impressed when they saw him choose a statue of his patron god. They then told him to choose something else as well. He then loaded his aged father Anchises, who was unable to follow them, on his back. Moved, the Achaeans in honour of this pious hero, allowed him to take all the rest of his possessions as well. The myth goes on to say that Aeneas reached Italy where he founded Rome or that he lived there and that it was founded later by his descendant Romulus.

death from this meeting, bared her breast to accept the blow from her betrayed husband. But Menelaus' sword clattered to the floor, and husband and wife were reunited with a kiss. Menelaus took Helen away with him - and once more this fateful woman, on whose behalf a war that shook the known world had been fought, ended up as the winner of the game.

When Laocoon discovered that the horse was hollow, snakes sent by Athena crushed him and his sons in their coils. (Laocoon group, 1st century B.C., Rome, The Vatican),

The Heroes Return

Ilium, as the acropolis of Troy was also known, had fallen to the cunning of Odysseus, just as the gods had decided. The surviving heroes of the war now set out on the journey home. Menelaus and Helen went back to their palace in Sparta, where, ten years later, they were visited by Telemachus, son of Odysseus, who was in search of his father. A whole decade had passed, and Odysseus had not yet returned to Ithaca. Agamemnon, commander-in-chief of the Greek forces, came to a bloody end. It may have been that the curse of the Atreides, which had weighed so heavily on the royal house for so long, now burst upon him with all its strength. Clytemnestra, his wife, was involved in an affair with Aegisthus, his cousin. When Agamemnon returned to Mycenae, Clytemnestra killed him in his bath - and she, the faithless and murderous wife, was in turn killed with her lover Aegisthus by Orestes, son of Agamemnon and Clytemnestra. Ajax of Locris met his end in a shipwreck on the way home, while Diomedes and Idomeneus spent years in exile in southern Italy. Very few of the heroes were

Orestes killing the lover of his mother to avenge the murder of his father. (Black-figured amphora, London, British Museum).

The tragic figure of Cassandra, the daughter of Priam, also followed the dictates of her fate after the war. She was given as captive to Agamemnon to whom she bore two twin sons. When Agamemnon returned to Mycenae he took her with him arousing the jealousy of Clytemnestra who murdered him along with his wife.

Orestes received an order from Apollo to take revenge for his father and to kill Clytemnestra and Aegisthus. According to Sophocles, his sister Electra exhorted him to take revenge and Apollo gave his approval.
Before he arrived at Argos, Orestes started the rumour that he had been killed. Thus, with seemingly nothing to fear, Clytemnestra called Aegisthus to the palace where Orestes first killed his uncle and then his mother, despite the pleas of the latter.

Orestes at the exhortation of Electra kills his mother Clytemnestra. (Bronze lamina circa 570 B.C., Olympia, Archaeological Museum).

able to pick up their lives where they had left off. Among them was wise old king Nestor, who went back to Pylos and reigned in peace for the rest of his life.

What, then, of the man who captured Troy, the cunning, Odysseus, who could turn his hand to anything? Unfortunately, the gods had determined that his fate would be a strange one. In the end, he would come home to Ithaca, to his family and kingdom, but only after adventure upon adventure and after risking his life countless times. Homer has left us the superb epic in which we are told of Odysseus' wanderings: The Odyssey.

Odysseus and Diomedes shown in a somewhat cartoonish manner falling upon the Trojan spy Dolonus. (Lucian krater, 380 B.C., London, British Museum).

Clytemnestra having already been stabbed once, tries to escape from Orestes who is bent on revenge. (Silver, gilt seal, beginning of the 4th century B.C., Ioannina, Archaeological Museum).

5

THE ODYSSEY

THE WANDERINGS OF ODYSSEUS
THE RETURN TO ITHACA

After Homer in *The Iliad* related the story of the war that shook all of Greece in mythical times, he went on to narrate *The Odyssey*. Many experts consider this work by Homer to be more nature containing the adventures of Odysseus, the captor of Troy, from the time he left Troy to the moment he reached his home in Ithaca. During our time, the word "Odyssey" has come to mean precisely that: a series of seemingly endless vicissitudes experienced by everyone in his life, taken from the work of Homer which describes the wanderings and the tricks of a great hero. Odysseus, endowed with incredible abilities, both intellectual and physical, and imbued with the immortal spirit of the Greek race, set off with an entire fleet to at last arrive at his longed for island alone, exhausted and replete with experience. His yearning for Ithaca kept alive the flame of his desire for return to the point that the word "Ithaca" has come to mean a "great passion",

the goal and its pursuit, the dream that each person sets out to capture.

During his wanderings Odysseus sometimes found himself in inhospitable lands with barbarous peoples and strange creatures and other times in places where he was well-received and offered assistance.

He knew all the difficulties that beset the navy of his day: turbulent currents and dangerous passages, inhospitable harbours and fearsome inhabitants. He overcame them all with his persistence and his courage seeking out his fate and his destiny. He even went down to the underworld which very few mortals have ever visited. The people and the gods who welcomed him, loved him, to the point they wanted to keep him there, far from his beloved Ithaca.

His strange fate made it so he returned home alone and on a foreign ship after starting with an entire fleet and crew. But let us follow him on his long journey of return.

THE WANDERINGS OF ODYSSEUS

The Cicones and the Lotus-Eaters

After the destruction of Troy, Odysseus set out for home with Agamemnon's fleet, but the ships were scattered in a storm. Odysseus ran aground on the coast of Thrace, where the Cicones lived. They were allies of Troy, and so Odysseus overcame and looted Ismarus, one of their cities, sparing only Maron, the priest of Apollo, who made him a gift of twelve jars of sweet intoxicating wine. The landing and the attack on the city of the Cicones cost Odysseus the lives of six men from each of his ships. Now they sailed south again, to the sea of Cythera, near Cape Maleas. Their next stop was an island off the coast of Africa. The people of the country welcomed Odysseus and his companions when they landed to reconnoitre, offering them the lotus fruit which they themselves ate. But when the sailors of the ships of Odysseus ate the fruit they forgot their homelands and their wish to return there. In the end, Odysseus had to use force to get them to re-embark.

In the Country of the Cyclops

Odysseus' little fleet now sailed north and anchored at an island called the country of the Cyclops, which has been tentatively identified as Sicily. When they landed, Odysseus took with him twelve of his companions and bags of the wine of Maron as a gift to any people they might meet. On their way into the interior of the island, they came to a cave. Inside were huge quantities of fresh milk and cheese. Odysseus was so curious about the size of all the objects lying about that he paid no heed to the warnings of his companions, who wanted to leave. His desire was to see exactly how large was the being that lived in the cave. When the owner of the cave, the Cyclops Polyphemus, came home, he saw the strangers and imprisoned them in the cave by blocking its mouth with a boulder so large fifty men could not have moved it. He set to and devoured two of Odysseus' companions on the spot, and continued to eat them in pairs. Odysseus then offered him some of the wine of Maron. Polyphemus drank quite a lot of it with pleasure, and in a much merrier mood he asked Odysseus what his name might be. "My name is Noman", came the hero's answer.

The Cyclops of Sicily were a population of giants with supernatural powers. They had one eye and tended their herds. They lived in caves, did not form societies, were cannibals and did not have knowledge of viniculture or even wine. They were only occupied with their sheep.

The previous page:
Odysseus with his intelligence and his daring manages to drive a pointed stick into the eye of the Cyclops Polyphemus. (Proto-Attican krater, circa 670 B.C., Eleusis, Archaeological Museum).

In order to repay Odysseus for the fine wine, Polyphemus promised to devour him last.

Odysseus racked his brains for some way of escaping from the clutches of this cannibal beast. His first idea was to kill Polyphemus. But then who would move the rock across the mouth of the cave? And so he decided to blind the giant. Polyphemus, drunk, had sunk into a deep sleep. Odysseus and his surviving companions found a pointed stick in the cave. They heated it in the fire to make it as effective as possible, and then plunged it into the giant's one and only eye. The cries of Polyphemus in the night shook the island. The other Cyclops answered, calling out to Polyphemus to tell them the name of the man who had blinded him. But when Polyphemus answered "Noman", they thought he must have gone mad, and returned to their own caves since "no man" had hurt him. In the morning, the blind Polyphemus searched in vain for those who had injured him. Odysseus and his companions escaped from the cave by clinging to the thick wool on the bellies of the sheep of Polyphemus' flock. When they got back to their ships, had raised the sails and were ready to depart, Odysseus called out to Polyphemus that if he were ever asked again who had blinded him, he was to say "Odysseus, the spoiler of cities". In his rage, Polyphemus hurled huge boulders at the ships, but in vain. By now Odysseus' little fleet was out in the open sea. Polyphemus called on Poseidon, his father, to help him take his revenge - and this was the beginning of the wrath which the powerful god of the sea felt for Odysseus, and the start of a new round of troubles.

Polyphemus was the most savage of all the Cyclops. An oracle had told him that he would be blinded by Odysseus and the fact that he was deceived made him very angry. A much later myth relates his persual of the Nereid Galatea who was in love with Acis; he was killed by Polyphemus who crushed him with a rock.

Odysseus escaping from the cave of the Cyclops tied under the belly of a ram.

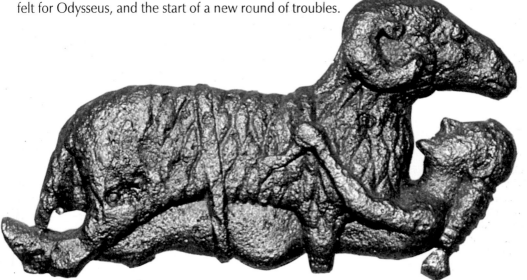

Odysseus blinding the unsuspecting giant Polyphemus. (Black-figured oinochoe, circa 500 B.C., Paris, The Louvre).

Aiolus, King of the Winds, leads the dance of the clouds and the Breezes (460-440 B.C.) Athenian vase

On the Island of Aeolus

The next stop after the country of Polyphemus was the island of Aeolus, master of the winds. Aeolus made Odysseus and his companions welcome, and gave them hospitality for a month. When the time came for them to leave, he presented Odysseus with a priceless gift: a bag made of ox-leather in which he had shut up all the strong winds. Only one wind had been left free: the breeze Zephyr, which would blow gently and take the ships straight home to Ithaca. Odysseus passed on to his companions Aeolus' warning that the bag was not to be opened because the winds would escape and blow them into great dangers on the rest of their voyage.

But the crew did not obey their master. They thought Aeolus had given Odysseus a bag of rare wine - and so when Odysseus was asleep one night someone opened the bag. Out rushed the howling winds. The little ship spun round and round like a nutshell in the fearsome storm. The gale blew them back to the island of Aeolus, but it was in vain that Odysseus begged Aeolus to send them another tail-wind; he was convinced now that the gods did not want to help Odysseus, so he left him to his fate.

The Island of Circe

Sailing on now as the winds might take them, Odysseus and his crew reached the country of the Laestrygonians, who were fierce eaters of human flesh. They escaped by the skin of their teeth from the cannibals, who pursued them with stones and sank all but one of their ships. This last craft and its crew were all that Odysseus had left when he sailed north again, to the island of Circe. The island where the witch Circe lived, called Aea, is now the headland of Monte Circeo, to the south of Latium. Circe was the sister of Aeëtes, the king of Colchis whom we have already met in the myths about the Argonauts and Pasiphae, wife of Minos of Crete.

To begin with, Circe welcomed the detachment which Odysseus sent out to reconnoitre under Eurylochus. But after serving them a banquet she began to touch them with her magic wand and turn them into swine and other animals. Eurylochus managed to escape and brought news to Odysseus of what was happening. He decided to go to meet the witch, to persuade her to give his sailors their human form once more. At first, Circe tried the same trick on Odysseus, but he proved invulnerable to her charms - thanks to a magic potion which Hermes had given him before he approached the palace. Odysseus threatened Circe with his sword and extracted from her a promise, under oath, that she would harm none of the company. The rest of their stay on the island was pleasant. During it, on Circe's advice, Odysseus descended into the underworld to ask the soul of Tiresias, the seer, about his return home. Tiresias told him he would have to go home alone, on a strange ship, and that he would be avenged on the suitors who wished to marry his wife. Apart from Tiresias, Odysseus also met the shades of many of his fellow-warriors who had been killed at Troy, together with a long list of famous people who dwelt in the underworld. Homer describes the lives in Hades of many of those sentenced to perpetual exemplary punishment there, including Sisyphus, Tantalus and the Danaids.

Circe prepares the magical potion for Odysseus, while one of his transformed companions watches uneasily.

Black-figured cylix showing Odysseus arriving in a threatening manner from the left to save his companions who have already been transformed.
(Circa 550 B.C., Boston).

155

Scylla

The Island of the Sirens - Scylla and Charybdis

The Sirens, whom we have met before - in the story of the Argonauts - were the next threat in store on Odysseus' voyage. In order to prevent his sailors from being overcome by the song of these evil spirits, who were half-women and half-birds, the wily Odysseus blocked up his companions' ears with wax. But he himself was curious to hear what the song of the Sirens sounded like. So he ordered the crew to lash him to the mast of the ship, where he could listen without endangering anyone. He told the sailors that if he should attempt to tell them in sign language to set him free, they were to bind him still tighter. And so matters fell out.

The *Sirens* were sea spirits. Their body from the waist up was female and the rest that of a bird. The Sirens are also to be found in the Argonaut campaign. They played the lyre, flute and also sang. Their song was so bewitching they drove travellers mad, who then approached their shores to have their ships deshed upon the sharp rocks, after which the people were devoured by the Sirens.

*Etruscan relief which depicts
Odysseus with his comapnions
passing the island of the Sirens.
(2nd century B.C.,
Paris, The Louvre).*

*"The Island of the Sirens"
a wood- carving by the Greek
painter and engraver
K. Grammatopoulos.*

After passing the island of the magical Sirens, Odysseus next had to deal with the Clashing Rocks and the channel between Scylla and Charybdis. Scylla was a sea monster which resembled a woman from the waist up, the remainder being composed of six fierce and monstrous dogs. She lived in a cave on the Italian side of the Strait of Messina, and she devoured passing sailors.

Just opposite, on the other side of the strait which separates Italy from Sicily, was Charybdis. This gigantic mon-

Odysseus bound, listens with bated breath to the sweet sounds of the lyre and the flute while dolphins leap up and dive back into the water.
(Back-figured lecythus, circa 500 B.C., Athens, Archaeological Museum).

ster swallowed vast quantities of sea water three times a day, sweeping down her throat anything which happened to be floating past on the sea, including ships. Then she regurgitated the water she had swallowed. These monsters made the Strait of Messina an extremely dangerous place, because it was not possible to avoid both of them. In the end, Odysseus sailed closer to Scylla so as not to be swallowed by Charybdis, and she devoured some of his sailors.

Scylla. (Relief of the 5th century B.C., found on Milos. London, British Museum).

The Oxen of the Sun -
The Island of Calypso

The island of Thrinacia was Odysseus' next stop. Here there were herds of white oxen sacred to the Sun. The winds prevented the companions from sailing on and their supplies had run out. Odysseus had strictly forbidden the sailors to slaughter and eat the sacred oxen of the Sun, but they disobeyed him and, in their hunger, killed and roasted some.

Helios, the sun god, demanded that Zeus punish Odysseus for this insult. As soon as the companions set out on their voyage once more, their ship ran into a storm, was struck by one of Zeus' thunderbolts, and sank. Only Odysseus, who had refused to eat any of the meat of the sacred oxen, was saved, clinging to the mast of the ship. The current swept him towards Charybdis, from whom he was saved at the last moment; just as she opened her mouth to suck in the water, Odysseus caught hold of a fig tree whose roots were deep in the rock. He was battered by the waves for nine whole days before being washed up on the shores of Ogygia, the island of Calypso. It was thus as a castaway that Calypso found him. She was a nymph, the daughter of Atlas, and she lived in a deep and beauti-

Many have expressed the view the view that the woman with the beautifully embroidered garments, who is conversing with Hermes, is none other than the Nymph Calypso. (Detail from a "Milian" amphora, circa 600 B.C., Athens, Archaeological Museum).

fully decorated cave which led out into wonderful gardens and forests. Odysseus spent an enchanted time with Calypso. She did everything in her power to keep him by her - even going so far as to promise him immortality. But his desire to go home would not fade in his heart; and one day Zeus, on the request of Athena, sent Hermes to beg Calypso to let Odysseus go home at last. Calypso even helped Odysseus find the wood he needed to make a raft, and provided him with supplies and advice for the journey.

On the Island of the Phaeacians

alypso sadly bade Odysseus farewell, and he set off in an easterly direction. But the wrath of Poseidon had not yet died away. He blew up mountainous waves, wrecked Odysseus' raft, and cast him into the sea once more. After hours of struggle with death among the wreckage of his raft, Odysseus, son of Laertes, was washed ashore, exhausted, on the island of the Phaeacians, now called Corfu (but which Homer terms Scheria). In his exhaustion, he fell asleep, but was wakened by girlish voices. It was Nausicaa, daughter of king Alcinous and queen Arete, rulers of the island, with the maidens of the palace. The girls had come to a nearby stream to wash clothes. When Nausicaa saw the stranger, she helped him up, gave him clothes to wear and - when he had washed in the river and stood before her looking as handsome as only Homer could describe - she showed him the way to her father's palace. So as not to set tongues wagging, she and her girls went home separately.

Alcinous and Arete welcomed Odysseus very warmly, and held a feast in his honour. He told them of all his adventures and hardships. They expressed their sympathy, their admiration of his feats, which had made him famous everywhere, and their desire that he should stay with them and marry Nausicaa. But Odysseus politely explained that he was longing for his home, Ithaca, and that he looked forward only to the day when he would see the smoke rising from the chimney of his house, even from a distance. When they heard that, the king and queen were so moved that they lent him a ship to take him to Ithaca. On the way, Odysseus fell asleep. The Phaeacians set him ashore on a quiet beach on Ithaca, surrounded by the gifts of Alcinous. The time set by the gods had come for Odysseus to set foot on his home island, after an absence of twenty years.

"And now Odysseus, dousing in the river,
....
scrubbed the coat of brine from back and shoulders and rinsed the clot of seaspume from his hair; got himself all rubbed down, from head to foot, then he put on the clothes the princess gave him. Athena lent a hand, making him seem taller, and massive too, with crisping hair in curls like petals of wild hyacinth, but all red-golden. Think of gold infused on silver by a craftsman, whose fine art Hephaestus taught him, or Athena: one whose work moves to delight: just so she lavished beauty over Odysseus' head and shoulders".

(Homer, The Odyssey, Book Six, 224-235, trans. E. Fitzgerald)

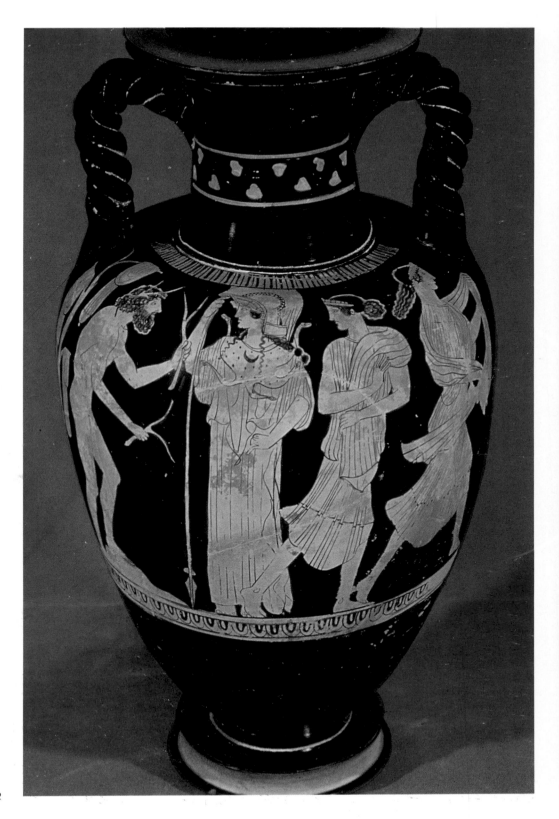

Odysseus in Ithaca

The years and the hardships had changed the son of Laertes. But what he had lost in youthfulness he had gained in experience and maturity. The grace and support of the goddess Athena had kept him handsome and strong. But no one recognised him - not even his wife Penelope, who had remained faithful to him. Over the years of his absence, much had changed. Odysseus' son Telemachus had grown to manhood, and had set off to seek out those with whom his father had fought at Troy, in the hope that they might know his whereabouts.

Odysseus went first to the hut of Eumaeus, his swineherd, in whom he had complete trust. Once Eumeaus had recognised him, Odysseus met Telemachus and learned about what had been happening at the palace. The suitors who wished to marry Penelope - and thus ascend the throne - had gathered from all over Ithaca and the other lands over which Odysseus held sway. They had installed themselves in the palace, eating and drinking at Odysseus' expense and squandering his fortune. Penelope had initially been able to keep them at bay by a trick, telling them that she would make her choice as soon as she had finished weaving a shroud for her father-in-law, old Laertes, which

Euryclea, the nurse of Odysseus, was the first one to recognize him. Washing the feet of the "stranger" she saw on his foot the old scar the son of Laertes had received from a wild boar when he had gone hunting with his grandfather as a boy. The dedicated nurse did not say anything right away, but first took the good news to Penelope.

On the opposite page: Odysseus, under the protective eye of Athena and holding branches of supplication, approaches Nausicaa, the daughter of the king.

Design which shows the old woman Euryclea recognizing Odysseus seeing the old scar on his foot while Eumaeus who led Odysseus to the palace now offers him a gift. (From a red-figured cup: a vessel with two handles ("scyphos"), circa 400 B.C.).

she was making on her loom. Penelope wove all day - but at night, in secret, she undid what she had woven. In the end, the secret got out, and now eight of the suitors were becoming more insistent and the queen had been forced into a corner. She was under pressure from all sides to make up her mind as to which suitor she would marry. When Odysseus found out about all this, he decided to teach them a lesson they would never forget. He disguised himself as a beggar and entered the palace with Telemachus. No one recognised him, except Argus, his faithful dog, who had been merely a puppy when Odysseus set off for Troy. As soon as he saw his master, Argus climbed to his feet, lay down in front of Odysseus, wagged his tail, and died.

Odysseus Takes Revenge on the Suitors

The sudden appearance of this unknown beggar, asking for food, caused the suitors to behave roughly towards him. When she was told that a stranger had turned up, Penelope was the only person who wanted to talk to him - in case he had some news of her

Odysseus pulls back his bow against the suitors. (Detail from a red-figured scyphos, circa 450 B.C., Berlin).

husband. Odysseus did not reveal himself to her, but he raised her hopes that Odysseus would be coming soon. Penelope, however, was unwilling to believe him, and so she announced that the suitors would compete against each others in games. She would marry the winner. The archery contest required considerable skill on the part of the competitors - not least because first they had to bend the bow of Odysseus himself, which Penelope had kept safe. Then they had to shoot the arrow through the holes in a number of axes set in a line. One after another the suitors tried, but they all failed even to bend the bow. In the end, Odysseus asked if he could try. With amazement, the suitors saw him bend the bow easily and hit the target effortlessly with his first shot. The hour of reckoning had come. Odysseus' devoted servants locked all the palace doors and the king and his son Telemachus picked up the weapons which they had left earlier in an upper room. The slaughter of the suitors followed. Word came to Penelope in her apartments, and she hardly dared believe that her husband had come home. In the end, he convinced her of his identity by revealing secrets that only the two of them knew, and by describing her bridal chamber.

In this design Penelope is shown sitting sadly before her loom while her son Telemachus looks at her thoughtfully.

Epilogue

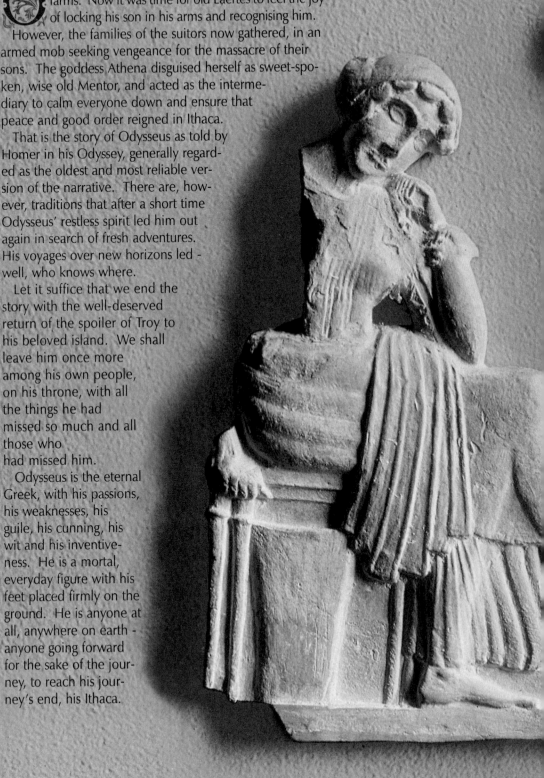

On the following day, Odysseus looked round his farms. Now it was time for old Laertes to feel the joy of locking his son in his arms and recognising him.

However, the families of the suitors now gathered, in an armed mob seeking vengeance for the massacre of their sons. The goddess Athena disguised herself as sweet-spoken, wise old Mentor, and acted as the intermediary to calm everyone down and ensure that peace and good order reigned in Ithaca.

That is the story of Odysseus as told by Homer in his Odyssey, generally regarded as the oldest and most reliable version of the narrative. There are, however, traditions that after a short time Odysseus' restless spirit led him out again in search of fresh adventures. His voyages over new horizons led - well, who knows where.

Let it suffice that we end the story with the well-deserved return of the spoiler of Troy to his beloved island. We shall leave him once more among his own people, on his throne, with all the things he had missed so much and all those who had missed him.

Odysseus is the eternal Greek, with his passions, his weaknesses, his guile, his cunning, his wit and his inventiveness. He is a mortal, everyday figure with his feet placed firmly on the ground. He is anyone at all, anywhere on earth - anyone going forward for the sake of the journey, to reach his journey's end, his Ithaca.

Homer was the greatest poet of all time. We know little of his life, not even precisely where he came from. Seven towns have vied for this honor: Smyrna, Rhodes, Colophon, Salamis on Cyprus, Chios, Argos and Athens. Smyrna is considered the most likely as there are many Ioanian elements in his work. The poet lived during the 9th century B.C. His immortal epics, The Iliad and The Odyssey are the oldest and finest works of literature in the world while many others are also attributed to him. Many writers believe he lived at the time of the Trojan War while others maintain he came after it. Homer died on the island of Ios and was buried there like a hero with sacrifices and dedications in his honor. The detailed descriptions in his work of the life and the cultural leved of the Greeks during his period, are the golden legacy of Greece and the rest of the world.

Odysseus and Penelope at the moment of their meeting, she seated holding her head in despair in her hand while he dressed as an unfortunate beggar kneels before her.
(Milian relief circa 460-450 B.C., Paris, The Louvre).

A Final Word

We hope that in this brief work we have managed to present both a concise and yet comprehensive picture of Greek Mythology. Myths, whether religious, historical or didactic and beyond any truth they may contain, show us the development of human thought. In its entirety mythology is an inexhaustible source from which can be drawn material for endless texts. Many of the figures we mention simply as names in the various chapters and sections have their own myth, perhaps less well-known but nevertheless interesting and unique.

Here it should be stressed that there are a number of versions of the same myth depending on the area in which each thrived. We selected the best known of these variations which are also the ones that have prevailed.

What is of particular interest here is that in the total number of narrations, there are many events that do not have a logical place in time. Myths referring to the same subject and which have survived separately, speak of the same matters and yet they appear to have taken

Before the "End"

place at different times. Heroes, for example, live the events of one period, while in another text it is related that these events were acted out during a time when the heroes themselves were elsewhere. So, we must accept that myths have a very flexible time frame. Furthermore, our far-off ancestors when they were making their world and taking their first, important steps in the evolution of mankind, had no idea that we would all be so involved with these experiences so many years later. Otherise — who can say? — they might have tried to fill in all the empty spaces they left, against their will, for the students of today who are trying to find the truth in the so distant past.

But what remains of unquestioned importance, is the fact that from those distant centuries have survived written testimony, objects and above all else works of rare art which prove the existence of everything we have set forth. Whether you come across them in Greece, their homeland, or in the great museums of the world, ask them. They have so much to tell you!

Our Bibliography

Our sources for this brief and, we hope, comprehensible presentation, are taken from ancient Greek literature and a number of eminent writers from that time are mentioned in our text: Hesiod, Homer, Apollodorus, Apollonius of Rhodes, Strabo, Plutarch, Pausanias, Pindar, Theocritus, Euripides, Sophocles, Aeschylus, and Lucian to name but a few. We took valuable information and analyses from the modern studies of K. Kerenoi, I. Karkides, Rispen and Pierre Fkrimal.

This book is not designed to take a special place in international bibliography and should not be judged on such a basis.

There are many Greek and froeign experts who have already done honour to this area. This book aims for simplicity and cogency in its treatment of the subjects of Greek mythology, full of love and respect for its sources. We feel that Greek mythology is of universal value and that is why people everywhere should become familiar with it.

Index

Acastus....................103
Aceso 53
Acrisius................ 104,106
Actaeon 38
Acheron....................55
Achilles..........127,131,134,135
..............136,138,139,140,141
Ademete....................74
Ademetus....................74
Adonis......................44
Adrastis...................118
Aea.......................155
Aeacus....................126
Aegeas.............. 82,87,89
Aeetes............54,96,100,102
Aegistus.............. 123,146
Aegle......................53
Aemon....................119
Aeneaus..................44,144
Aeolia....................155
Aeropi....................123
Aesacus...................129
Aeson......................95
Aethra..................92,84
Agamemnon........ 122,123,130,
..................132,134,138,146
Agave.....................114
Agenoras..................26,114
Aglaea.....................47
Aithras....................10
Ajax................. 129,131,136,
.... 140,141,145
Alcemene................64,66
Alcestes...................73
Alcinous..................163
Alcyone....................12
Amaltheia..................24
Amazons....................74
Amphitrite.................32
Amphitryonus...............64
Anagi......................60
Anchyses..................44,144
Androgeos..................88
Andromache.......... 140,144
Andromeda.................106
Anteaus............... 10,76
Anteia....................108
Anticleia.................165
Antigone............... 116,118,119

Anticleia 165
Antilochus............... 138
Aphrodite............42,43,44,127
Apollo................36,37,40
Apsyrtus.................100,102
Arachni....................31
Ares.................30,42,45
Arete.....................163
Argonauts................96,98
Argos................ 40,164
Argo..................96,97,98
Ariadne.................52,88
Arisbe....................129
Aristaeus................37,38
Arpalycus..................40
Artemis............. 38,39,132
Archelaus..................79
Asclepius................37,53
Asia......................10
Assaracus.................129
Asteria...................10
Asterope...................12
Ate.......................60
Athamas.............50,94,95
Athena.............14,29,30
................77,127,162,165
Atlantis...................12
Atlas................12,76,77
Atreas...................122,123
Atreids...................122
Augeas...................72,73
Autolycus..................40
Avgi.............. 54,109
Avderos....................40

Bacchus, see Dionysus.........50,
....................51,52
Bellerophon.................108,109
Bia........................23
Breseis..................134,138

Cabiri.....................24
Cadmus............. 26,45,114
Calchas..........61,132,133
Calliope...................37
Callirrhoe................129
Calypso..................163,164
Cancer.....................69
Cassandra........37,129,144,146

Castalia 61
Caucasus 16
Cecrops 31
Celaeno 11,12
Celeus 34
Centaurs 95
Cerberus 78,79
Cercyon 87
Ceto......................11
Chaos 47
Charon.....................55
Charybdis 160-162
Chiron 95,96
Chelon 40
Chthonophile 40
Chimera 108
Chrysaor 33
Chryseida 134
Chrses 134
Chrysippus 120
Chrysotheme...............123
Cithairon................66,114
Cicones 152
Circe.................54,157
Cleopatra.................129
Clymene 10,40
Clytemnestra 123,146
Coeus 10
Corybantes 24,52
Coronis 37
Couretes 24
Cranaus...................31
Cratos....................23
Creius....................10
Creon 67,116,117,
.... 118,119
Creousa...................129
Cronus 10,11,12,15,152
Cyzicus 98
Cyclops.............10,11,12,13,15
.... 152,153,154
Cycnus....................45
Cyparrisus 37
Cyrene 37,38

Daedalus..................110
Danae 104,105
Danaedes 112,155
Dardanus..................129

171

Daphne......................37
Day..........................10
Deimus.....................44
Denaneira..............79,80
Deiphobus...........129,144
Demeter................34,35
Dicte....................105,106
Diomedes.......45,73,131,142
Diomede..................134
Dione......................42
Dionysus (Sacchus)...25,50,51,
...........................52,91
Dioscuri...................103
Doliones..................98
Doris....................11,32

Earth..................10,11,13
Echidna...................120
Echo.....................56,57
Eileithyia..................25
Enceladus.................29
Electra................12,54,123
Epimetheus...............6,18
Epione.....................53
Eridanas...............102,113
Erichthinius...............47
Eris........................60
Erinnyes...................59
Eros.....................44,58
Eteoclis.............116,118,119
Eumaeus..................165
Euryale..................11,33
Eurybia..................10,11
Eurycleia..................166
Eurylochus................157
Eurynome...............46,108
Eurystheas.............27,28,
...........................77,122
Eurytus...................80
Europa..................26,27

Galateia..................152
Ganymede..............25,129
Geryon.....................74
Giants................13,14,15
Glaucus........59,109,140,142
Gorgon.......53,106,107,109
Graces....................42
Graiae..................11,104
Gratonus..................28

Hades..............34,35,54,112
Harpies..................11,91
Harmony................44,45
Hebe....................25,60
Hecate.....................11
Hecuba...............140,144
Hector.........129,133,138,139
Helios...................34,54
Helen................130,144,145
Hellen.....................19
Hermaphrodite............47
Hermes.........18,40,41,44,154
Hermione..................135
Hesperides..............12,76
Hestia.....................47
Hera...................18,28,46,
...........................47,127
Heracles................14,64-80
Hesione..................67,139
Hephaestus..............42,46
Hippolochus..............109
Hippolyte..................74
Hippolytus.................92
Hours (Horae)..........25,28,59
Hubris.....................60
Hyacinth...................37
Hygeia.....................53
Hylas....................96,99
Hymen.....................37
Hyperion................10,54

Iacchus..................60,61
Iapetus....................10
Iaso.......................53
Icarus.....................110
Idas.....................96,131
Idomeneas.................131
Ino......................50,194
Io........................28,40
Iobates................108,109
Iolaos.....................69
Ioli.......................80
Iris.....................54,130
Isandrus..................109
Ismene................116,119
Iphigeneia...........123,132,133
Iphicles...................66
Jocasta.............114,116,118
Jason........95,96,97,98,99,100
...........................102,103

Labdacus.................114
Laertes.................130,169
Laestrygines..............157
Laius.................114,115,120
Laodameia.................109
Laocoon...................144
Laodice...................129
Laomedon..................67
Lernaean Hydra...........69
Leto.....................25,36
Lichas.....................80
Linus......................37
Lites......................60
Lotus-Eaters..............152

Machaonas.................53
Maenads...................52
Maia..................12,25,40
Marsyas.................48,52
Maronas..................152
Medea.....................67
Megara....................67
Medusa..................11,53
Melantheia................19
Melo nippe................74
Melaegrus...............45,79
Menelaus.........123,130,140,
...........................144,145
Menoetius.................10
Mentiras..................166
Merope...............12,114,115
Metida....................29
Midas.....................50
Minos..............26,73,88,111
Minotaur................88,91
Mnemosyne.............10,25
Moires (Fates).........25,58
Muses.....................25
Mopsus....................96
Mymidons.............126,134
Myrtilus...................40

Narcissus..................57
Naucrate..................110
Nausicaa..................163
Neleas.....................33
Nemesis...................60
Neoptolemus..........135,144
Nephele.................94,95
Nereus..................11,32

Nereids 11,141
Nessus...................................79
Nestor 148
Nike 23
Niceppe...............................122
Night....................................10
Niobe 38
Nisus...................................108

Oceanus 10,12,26
Odysseus.......130,131,144,148
...............................150-169
Oedipus..............114,115,116,
.................................117,118
Oenimaos.............................45
Ogygia 160
Orthe...................................12
Oeneas 50
Olympus 12,22
Orestes 123
Orion....................................53
Orpheus...........37,96,112,113
Ortygia................................36
Orthros 74,75,120

Palaemon 47
Palamedes...........................130
Pallas Athena 30
Pallas 14
Panacea 53
Pan.................................40,56
Pandora 18,19
Paris..................127,129,130,
.................................140,141
Pasiphae 54,88,157
Patroclus 135,138
Pegasus.............33,53,108,109
Peitho 60
Peleus.............................96,126
Penelope 164-167
Perithoos........................87,92
Pelias 33,95,96,103
Pelops................................122
Pelopids..............................123
Penthesilea.........................140
Periphetes 84
Perseus....................104-106
Persephone 34,35,55
Perses 10,54
Peuce 56

Pitheus.................82,84,122
Phaeton 113
Phaea...................................86
Phaeacians..........................163
Phaedra 92,93
Philoctetes 80,141
Philonisk..............................40
Phineus.................................99
Phoebe.................................12
Phobus.................................44
Pholus..................................95
Phorces 11
Phrixos.........................94,95,96
Pleiads 12
Pleione.................................12
Pleisthones 122
Pluto.....................34,35,55
Podaleirius............................55
Podarces 67,129
Pollux-Castor 96
Polybus...............40,114,115
Polydectes 105-106
Polydorus.....................115,129
Polynices.............116,118,119
Polyphemus............52,152-154
Polyxene 129,140
Pondus 11
Poseidon 29,30,32,33
Priam 129,139,140,144
Proerus..........................108,109
Procrustes............................87
Prometheus.................12,16,76
Proteus 59
Protosilaud.........................133
Protogenia............................19
Python.................................36
Pythian.............................36,61
Pyrrha.................................10

Radamanthys 26
Rhea...............................10,11,24

Sarpedon 26,109
Satyrs 32,48
Scheria................................163
Sciron..................................86
Scylla.............................160,161
Selene (Moon)...................10,57
Semele............................25,50
Sthenelus.............................122

Sines 85
Sintians................................46
Sirens 103,159
Sisyphus 55,60
Sleep...................................60
Solymi 108
Styx......................22,23,127
Symplegadea
(Clashing Rocks) 99
Sphinx 116,120

Talus 26,102,110
Tantalus 55
Tartarus 11,12
Taygete 12
Tiresias 61,117
Telemon...................67,96,129
Telemachus...130,146,163,167
Telephassa...........................26
Teucrus...............................129
Tethys 10,26,46
Thanatos (Death).............60,73
Thaumas 11,54
Theia 10,54
Themis...........................25,36,58
Theseus........82,83,84,85,86,87
.................88,89,90,91,92,93
Thetis 10,126,135,141
Thoosa.................................53
Thrinacia.............................160
Thyea..................................19
Thyestes 122,123
Titans 12,13
Titanesses 12
Triptolemus 35
Triton 33,59
Troax (Troy)........................129
Trojan horse.........142,143,144
Trilus 37,129
Tyehe..................................60
Tydeus................................119
Tyndareus...........................123
Typhon..........................14,120
Tyro 33

Zelus...................................23
Zeus............11,12,13,14,16,24,
.....................25,26,27,28,29

Gods & heroes
of GREEK
MYTHOLOGY
embellish a
New
deck of cards
just on the market

EDITIONS TOUBI'S
ΕΚΔΟΣΕΙΣ

The best gift from Greece

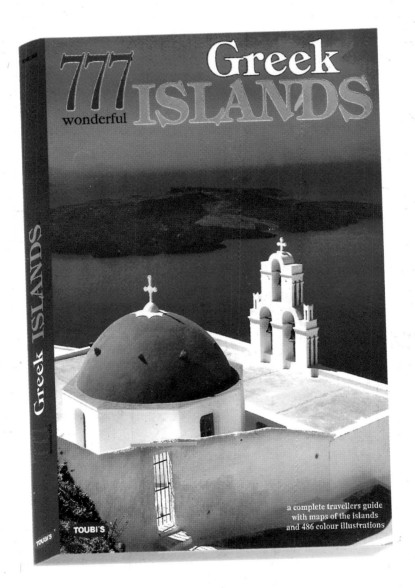

777 Greek Islands

Many years in preparation, now completed in 1994. A unique edition which treats **777** beautiful *Greek islands* from the 9,500 islands and rocky outcroppings of the *Greek Archipelago*.

Format: 17×24, Pages: 272
81 maps of the islands, 360 colour illustrations